COOK AHEAD

D1621223

By the same author

LEAVE IT TO COOK
NEVER TOO LATE

COOK
AHEAD

STELLA ATTERBURY

MACDONALD · LONDON

© 1970 Stella Atterbury

First published by
Macdonald & Co (Publishers) Ltd,
49/50 Poland St, London W.1
Made and printed in Great Britain by A. Wheaton & Co, Exeter

SBN 356 03053 9

CONTENTS

FOREWORD

IN my book *Never Too Late* I tell how my original cooking ideas enabled me, a middle-aged woman with little cooking experience but endless enthusiasm, to run, with success, the kitchen of our newly acquired country house hotel.

Now, after several years of retirement, with more experience, a still unexhausted fund of enthusiasm, and the cooperation of my daughter June Thompson, this book is written. Here we enlarge on earlier ideas, add new ones and many more recipes. My daughter, the mother of two teenage boys, naturally leads a much fuller and more active life than I, so we have borne in mind the stress of modern living and the tastes of three generations. We hope that this approach will help others as it has helped us to save time, effort and often money, yet be instrumental in serving varied dishes, both for entertaining and as an everyday routine.

Roast and casseroled dishes are not included here, as they and the Slow-Cooking Method are covered in my first book and enlarged upon in *Leave It To Cook* (Penguin).

S.A.

To
MARJORIE HESSELL TILTMAN

PERSONAL VIEWS ON EQUIPMENT

As for any other craft, cooking demands the best equipment the cook can afford – though the best is not always the most expensive. Equipment should do the job well, quickly and should not require excessive washing and drying after use. For small families and small quantities it is often quicker to use a good hand implement than its mechanical equivalent.

The following is not intended as a guide to those equipping a kitchen from scratch, but as an indication of what we consider the best tools for specific jobs.

Cooking and Serving
When a dish can be cooked and served in the one container, it is highly satisfactory to the cook. Therefore, invest in as many *oven and flame-proof casseroles and dishes* as possible. All the better if some of these can be non-stick as well.

Boiling
A *non-stick milk saucepan* is a time-saving joy for sauces as well as milk.

Frying
Non-stick frying pans are also a boon, especially if the non-stick surface is baked and bonded to the pan itself – these last longer and do not require such careful treatment. Frying pans should have lids but, failing lids of their own, these can be improvised from saucepan lids or well-fitting enamel plates.

It is useful to have three frying pans of different sizes, one of which should be a small (about seven inches) heavy pan to be kept exclusively for pancakes and omelettes.

For deep frying have a *chip pan and basket*, or just a basket to fit an existing saucepan.

Pressure Cooking
Some cooks swear by *pressure cookers*, others shun them in terror. We are very fond of ours, but do not use them indiscriminately. They are excellent for root and many other vegetables, for pastas, for turning poultry carcasses and bones into stock and are incomparable for making apple purée (p. 132).

Steaming
Steamers with perforated bottoms, that fit on top of pans of boiling water, are needed for steamed puddings, and are good for cooking root vegetables. Steamed or pressure-cooked potatoes are equally satisfactory. When steamed, they take longer to cook but have an advantage – their progress can be

1

watched and any potatoes that are cooked before the others can be removed.

Poaching

Poaching rings are a useful cheap investment. Eggs cooked in them are really poached – not steamed in butter as they are in so-called poaching pans.

Baking

Home-bakers should have:

A good selection of cake, flan and sandwich tins – a number of these with loose bottoms.

Alcan dishes and cases. We consider these aluminium foil cases an excellent innovation, see p. 39.

A roll of Bakewell. This excellent vegetable parchment prevents cakes and biscuits from sticking, and can be used several times.

Wire trays for cooling pastries, cakes and biscuits.

An extra baking sheet. The one sheet provided in most cookers is often inadequate, and a second one saves time and fuel.

Roasting

A meat thermometer, though not essential, we find a real aid to carefree roasting, and especially slow roasting.

Roasts wrapped in '*Look*', the transparent cooking film, retain their natural juices, and brown and crispen far better than when cooked in foil.

Cutting and Chopping

Cooks should have *several really good knives* and *an efficient sharpener* to keep a razor edge.

Sharp scissors are also needed in the kitchen. We have found that all-purpose household scissors or those intended for dressmaking are cheaper and likely to prove more reliable than some much publicized kitchen scissors.

Small scissors – nail scissors, for instance – are good for chopping up parsley, mint and other herbs, though we prefer a *Mouli-Parmint*.

Cooks who use garlic will find a *garlic press* a time saver.

Hand grating, shredding and slicing

There are excellent hand graters, shredders and slicers on the market. These, when used for small quantities, will take no longer to use and wash up than mechanical appliances.

A rectangular, stainless steel grater is most useful for little everyday jobs, and needs no setting up. 'Nutbrown' produces a good grater-cum-shredder with well defined cutters – fine, medium and coarse, not always found in other makes. When practical, press the food against the grater with the palm of the hand – this appears to be quicker and does save grated knuckles.

For bigger jobs, *Mouli-Julienne No. 2* is an asset. It has five different discs, will stand over a large plate, and packs up for storage. However, when food is grated, shredded or sliced on to a piece of kitchen paper, it handles more easily and washing up is reduced.

Elaborate gadgets can be bought for slicing beans, but will not be more efficient than the handy, cheap little *Zipp Bean Slicer*. This has been on the market for years, so let us hope it will not disappear. It is worth buying more than one of these inexpensive slicers, so that several members of the family can prepare beans at the same time.

Mincing   Most hand-operated mincing machines must be clamped to the table and require a lot of washing up. Mouli's *Moulinette* minces raw and cooked fish and meat very well, provided they are cut into small pieces. It is washed up in a moment, and is therefore a winner for smaller amounts but, when possible, have an electric mincer for larger quantities.

Draining,   For draining and straining you can rely on a roll of absorbent
Straining   kitchen paper, a colander and a set of plastic sieves. But for the
and   sieving of cooked foods it is much quicker to use the excellent
Sieving   *Moulin Legumes*, which is sold in two family sizes.

Blending   When possible, cooks should have electrically worked machines for blending. Perhaps the most essential of these is the *liquidizer*, as one cannot liquidize by hand. *Hand operated cream making machines* will do one of the jobs (i.e. emulsify milk and butter), but these are difficult to buy, and may disappear altogether now that liquidizers are so popular. For general blending, though desirable, *heavy standard machines* are not necessary. *Light, hand-held blenders* are excellent, and will do the same work. In fact, for quick blending of small quantities these hand-held machines may be preferable.

A good quality hand rotary whisk is needed by those with only a heavy standard mixer, or with no electric blender at all.

Cooks require *a selection of spoons* – wooden for blending and stirring, metal for folding, wire and perforated, e.g. a kitchama-jig, for beating, whisking, straining and working fat into flour.

Measuring   Reliable *kitchen scales* are essential for those who take their cooking seriously, and to be without them is a handicap. Yet with the approaching introduction of the Metric System, cooks with no scales may not feel like buying a pair which will soon become out of date. There are, however, *measures that indicate weight* – Tala makes a good one. These are not as accurate as scales and only apply to a limited number of ingredients, but are certainly useful.

A transparent – glass or plastic – pint measure with clearly marked fluid ounces is a must for all kitchens.

A set of measuring spoons is, we consider, another necessity, as household spoons vary to such an extent. Yet as *an ordinary tablespoon* is easier to manipulate, keep one which corresponds with the measuring spoon, specially for cooking.

Timing *Smiths Timers* save many burnt and overcooked dishes. They are needed by busy housewives who often undertake more than one job at a time.

Storing Cooking ahead requires a good selection of storage equipment – *Look, plastic bags* and *pudding basins with lids* for short-term storage – perishable food keeps considerably longer in *Tupperware. Airtight tins* are a necessity for pastries, cakes and biscuits.

WEIGHTS AND MEASURES

As the Metric system is shortly to be used in the United Kingdom the following rough and ready tables may be useful.

Avoirdupois Weight		*Metric Weight*
1 ounce (16 drams)	=	28·350 grams (say 28$\frac{1}{3}$ grams)
$\frac{1}{4}$ pound (4 oz)	=	0·113 kilogram
$\frac{1}{2}$ pound (8 oz)	=	0·22 kilogram (say $\frac{1}{4}$ kilo)
1 pound (16 oz)	=	0·453 kilogram (say $\frac{1}{2}$ kilo)

Capacity Measure

British		*Metric*	
1 gill (5 fluid oz)	=	1·42 decilitres	(say 1$\frac{1}{2}$ decil)
1 pint (20 fluid oz)	=	0·568 litre	(say $\frac{1}{2}$ litre)
1 quart (2 pints)	=	1·136 litre	(say 1 litre)
1 gallon (8 pints)	=	4·546 litre	(say 4$\frac{1}{2}$ litres)

Some American Measures

1 U.S. pint	=	16 fluid oz	1 British pint	=	20 fluid oz
		2$\frac{1}{2}$ U.S. pints	=	2 British pints	
		1 U.S. CUP	=	8 fluid oz	

CHEESE FOUNDATION

CHEESE is one of our staple foods, and is the main ingredient of many a hot dish. With a supply of Cheese Foundation, which is quick and simple to prepare, you can produce in a few moments varied cheese dishes, sauces, fillings and spreads. The Foundation will keep for a week or so in a cool larder and well over a month in a refrigerator.

The recipe is best made with a strong Cheddar type cheese. Stale oddments can however be used, and should these be too mild, the flavour will be improved by the inclusion of a little Parmesan. Beer also gives a pleasant tang, but some people and most children prefer the Foundation when milk is used.

For a household of 2 allow:

1 *egg*	6 *fluid oz beer or milk*
1 *dessert spoon dry mustard*	½ *lb grated cheese*
1 *teaspoon Worcester sauce*	½ *oz butter or margarine*

Place the egg in a medium-sized saucepan. Stir into it the mustard, sauce, liquid and cheese. Add the fat. Place pan over medium heat and stir until the mixture thickens. No need to worry – it never curdles.

Pour the Foundation into a container, cover when cold and use as wanted in any of the suggested recipes, or in others of your own invention.

Cheese Foundation Recipes

Cheese Sauce 1*

To make a good strong cheese sauce allow:

> *to any measured quantity of Cheese Foundation*
> ⅕ *to* ¼ *of that amount milk, Sour Cream (pp. 105, 106),*
> *beer or suitable stock*

Measure the Foundation and liquid in spoons into a small saucepan. Place over gentle heat and stir with a wooden spoon, until completely blended.

* *Cheese Sauce 2, p. 85, is made with Basic Cream Sauce.*

Savoury Egg Nests   Oven setting 400°F, Mark 6

For each serving allow:

>   *a piece of toast*   *1 egg*
>   *2 tablespoons Cheese Foundation*   *salt and pepper to taste*

Spread the Foundation on the toast, place on a baking sheet and put in the pre-heated oven.

Separate the eggs – the whites into a mixing bowl and the yolks dropped carefully into individual egg cups. Add seasoning to the whites and whisk until stiff. Take out the baking sheet. Pile whites equally on to the pieces of toast, making holes in the centre of each. Drop yolks into these holes and return sheet to the oven for a few minutes, until the whites begin to colour. Serve.

Cheese Eggs   Oven setting 450°F, Mark 8

To serve 2 allow:

3 hard boiled eggs   *1 tablespoon milk or 2 teaspoons milk*
5 tablespoons Cheese Foundation   *and 2 teaspoons tomato ketchup*
1 teaspoon chopped parsley or dried chervil

Slice the eggs thinly and place in an oven dish.

Measure the Cheese Foundation into a small saucepan and place over gentle heat. Add the liquid and blend with a wooden spoon. Add the parsley or chervil and pour the sauce over the eggs.

Either put the dish in the pre-heated oven or under the grill until sizzling hot and brown on top, and serve; or the dish can be stored until wanted and then baked or grilled just before serving.

Cheese Omelette

For best results, all omelettes, other than soufflé omelettes (p. 106), should be cooked and served individually. They should be cooked in a small non-stick frying pan, or one kept for the purpose, which is never washed, but rubbed clean after use with absorbent kitchen paper. Failing that, any small pan will do, provided it has first been 'proved'. To do this, sprinkle the pan liberally with salt, heat slowly until hot, then rub clean with kitchen paper.

For each cheese omelette allow:

> 2 *large eggs*
> 1 *dessertspoon water*
> *salt and pepper to taste*
>
> ½ *oz butter*
> 6 *teaspoons Cheese Foundation*

Beat eggs and water lightly together, then season to taste.

Heat the butter in the omelette pan until sizzling but not brown. Pour in the beaten eggs. As the eggs begin to set, move edges towards the centre with a fork, and at the same time tilt the pan quickly in all directions, so that the uncooked egg flows to the edges.

Using a teaspoon, drop about 6 little mounds of Cheese Foundation over the setting omelette. When the underneath is lightly browned and the top still slightly moist, fold in half in the pan and slide on to a warm plate. Serve immediately.

Welsh Rarebit

For each serving allow:

> 1 *slice toast*   2–3 *tablespoons Cheese Foundation*

Spread cheese on toast, making sure the crusts or edges are completely covered. Heat and brown, either under the grill or in the oven.

Buck Rarebit

This is *a Welsh Rarebit* served with *an egg* on top.

Either poach the egg while the Rarebit is under the grill, or bake it according to *Eggs en Cocotte* (p. 106), while the Rarebit is in the oven.

Celery Rarebit

To serve 2 allow:

> 1 *or 2 medium sized sticks of celery*
> 2 *slices of toast*
>
> 6 *tablespoons Cheese Foundation*
> *a little grated cheese*

Cut the celery into neat pieces. Boil in a little salted water until just soft.

Heat the Cheese Foundation in a pan over gentle heat. Mix in the celery.

Pour the mixture over the toast and top with a little finely grated cheese. Brown under a hot grill.

Macaroni Cheese 1*   Oven setting 400°F, Mark 6

To serve 2 allow:

> 3 *oz macaroni*   *breadcrumbs*
> 4 *heaped tablespoons Cheese Foundation*   *grated cheese*
> 1 *tablespoon milk*

Cook macaroni in about 2 pints of boiling, well salted water until tender (15–20 minutes).

While macaroni is cooking, heat the Cheese Foundation and milk in a flame-proof oven dish, or in a saucepan.

Strain macaroni, add to the sauce and mix well. When using a saucepan, transfer to a greased pie dish. Top with breadcrumbs and grated cheese.

Bake in a pre-heated oven for about 20 minutes, or if to be served immediately, brown under a hot grill.

The prepared dish can be stored in a refrigerator or a cool place for several days, to be baked just before serving.

Macaroni Cheese with Frankfurters or Sausages

To serve 2 allow:

> *Macaroni Cheese* (above)   4 *frankfurters or* 4 *cooked skinless*
>   *sausages*

Cut the frankfurters or sausages into 1 inch lengths and mix with the Macaroni and Cheese Sauce before the application of the crumb, cheese and margarine topping.

Macaroni Cheese and Eggs

To serve 2 allow:

> *Macaroni Cheese* (above)   2 *eggs*

Make two holes in the blended Macaroni and Cheese Sauce; break eggs one by one into an egg cup and tip each one into its hole.

Draw the macaroni mixture carefully over the eggs before applying the crumb, cheese and margarine topping.

This dish must be baked and not grilled.

* *Macaroni Cheese 2*, p. 96, is made with Basic Cream Sauce.

Macaroni Cheese with Eggs and Frankfurters or Sausages

For a really substantial dish, the two previous recipes can be combined, and again must be baked and not grilled.

Macaroni Cheese and Left-overs

Macaroni Cheese (p. 10)   *Left-over: roasts, casseroles, boiled ham or bacon*

This makes an appetizing dish. The meat is minced or chopped and added to the freshly cooked macaroni. Any *gravy* or *sauce* can be blended with the Cheese Foundation instead of the prescribed milk.

Sweetcorn and Sausage Savoury   Oven setting 475°F, Mark 7

To serve 3–4 allow:

7 *oz tin of sweetcorn kernels*   *a little milk, if needed*
3 *heaped tablespoons Cheese Foundation*   *brown breadcrumbs*
4 *or more cooked chipolatas or frankfurters* *a little grated cheese*
                                             a little butter or margarine

Strain the corn over a pint measure.

Put the Cheese Foundation into a flame-proof oven dish or a small saucepan and place over gentle heat. The recipe requires 2 fluid oz of liquid; if the sweetcorn liquor is not sufficient, make this up with milk, and pour into the warm cheese. Stir with a wooden spoon until blended, then remove from heat.

Cut up the chipolatas or frankfurters into 1 inch lengths and add these and the sweetcorn to the warm sauce. When using a pan, transfer the mixture to an oven dish. Cover with the crumbs and cheese and dot with butter or margarine. Place in pre-heated oven or store and bake later for about 20 minutes or until brown.

Croque Monsieur 1*

For each serving allow:

2 *slices of bread, crusts removed*   *a little French mustard* (*optional*)
2–3 *tablespoons Cheese Foundation*   *a little parsley*
1 *or 2 thick slices of cooked ham*

* *Croque Monsieur 2*, p. 67, is made with Basic Cream Sauce.

Spread one side of each piece of bread with the Cheese Foundation and make a sandwich with the ham and mustard as the filling.

Fry in plenty of hot lard or dripping or, if preferred, toast each side under the grill. Garnish with fried parsley.

Croque Monsieur can also be made with corned beef or luncheon meat.

Savoury Rice   Oven setting 425°F, Mark 7

This is an excellent dish and also a good way of using left-over rice; in fact, when cooking rice for other dishes, it is well worth while to cook an extra supply for a savoury rice in the near future.

HOW TO COOK RICE

There are quite a few methods for cooking rice, and one of the simplest is to pour long-grained rice into your largest container, nearly filled with fast-boiling salted water. Allow it to boil rapidly, uncovered, for exactly 11 minutes. Then strain it immediately in a large wire or nylon sieve – don't use a colander. The rice can now, if the grains are not quite separate, be held under a hot tap and tossed with a fork. Either serve immediately or place rice in a hot covered container, stir in about 1 tablespoon olive oil, and keep hot in the oven until required – it will not spoil.

Left over rice, with or without olive oil, will keep for several days in the refrigerator. It can then be used in recipes or, in a covered container, reheated in the oven. The rice to be reheated must contain a little olive oil.

For 2 servings of Savoury Rice allow:

about 8 tablespoons of cooked rice or 3 oz uncooked long grained rice	salt and pepper to taste
1 oz butter or margarine	1 tablespoon parsley, finely chopped (optional)
1 large or 2 small onions, finely sliced	brown breadcrumbs
4 heaped tablespoons Cheese Foundation	a little finely grated cheese a little extra butter or margarine

When uncooked rice is used, boil and strain this as given.

Place the fat in a small pan over gentle heat and, when melted, add the onion. Cook covered until the onion is soft and transparent but not brown. Remove from heat and work the Cheese Foundation into the onion and butter with a wooden spoon. When well blended, add the cooked rice, seasoning and parsley. Mix well, then transfer mixture to an oven dish. Cover top with crumbs and grated cheese, and dot with little dabs of butter.

When the dish is to be served immediately, it is now baked about 20–25 minutes in pre-heated oven, or if the ingredients are still warm, it can be browned under the grill.

When the savoury rice is wanted for some future date, the prepared dish can be stored in a refrigerator or a cool place for several days and baked just before serving.

Savoury Rice Variations

Savoury Rice with Frankfurters or Sausages
Savoury Rice and Eggs
Savoury Rice with Eggs and Frankfurters or Sausages
Savoury Rice and Left-overs

These dishes are prepared as given for Macaroni Cheese Variations (pp. 10–11), using Savoury Rice instead of Macaroni Cheese.

Leek and Ham Loaf   Oven Setting 375°F, Mark 5

To serve 3–4 allow:

1 *lb leeks*	1 *tablespoon sour cream or*
¼ *lb finely sliced cooked ham*	1 *tablespoon top milk and* ¼ *teaspoon*
about 6 *tablespoons Cheese*	*lemon juice (fresh or bottled)*
Foundation	5 *tablespoons fresh breadcrumbs*
brown breadcrumbs	1 *egg*
	a little grated cheese

Slice leeks lengthwise, then cut into 2 inch pieces. Either boil for 4 minutes in salted water, or pressure cook for 2½ minutes. Strain.

Well grease a loose-bottomed 6 inch cake tin. Line the bottom and sides of this with slices of ham which have been spread lavishly with Cheese Foundation and sprinkled with brown breadcrumbs. Place the spread sides against the tin. Chop up the remaining ham slices.

Measure 4 tablespoons of Cheese Foundation into a small pan and place over gentle heat until warm and pliable.

When top milk is used, measure this into a cup and stir in the lemon juice. This produces sour cream. Remove pan from heat and stir in the sour cream, using a wooden spoon. When well blended, add the leeks, cut up ham, fresh crumbs and the egg. Stir vigorously and spoon the mixture into the cake tin. Cover top with more brown crumbs and a little grated cheese.

Bake in pre-heated oven for 30 minutes or, when quite cold, store in a refrigerator or a cool place and cook later. When cooked, unmould and serve hot.

Ham and Pineapple au Gratin   Oven Setting 425°F, Mark 7

To serve 2 allow:

¼ *lb sliced cooked ham*
3 *slices tinned pineapple,*
  cut in two horizontally
4 *heaped tablespoons Cheese*
  Foundation
1 *tablespoon pineapple juice*

1 *tablespoon chopped parsley or dried*
  chervil
brown breadcrumbs
a little grated cheese
¼ *oz butter or margarine*

Cover the bottom of a greased oven dish with half the ham slices, lay the pineapple on top and cover with the rest of the ham.

Measure the Cheese Foundation into a small pan and place over gentle heat. Add the pineapple juice and work it into the cheese with a wooden spoon. Add the herbs and pour the mixture over the ham. Cover with crumbs and grated cheese and little dabs of butter or margarine.

Bake in pre-heated oven for 15–20 minutes or, when cold, store in a refrigerator or a cool place and cook later. Serve hot.

Ham Baked with Tomatoes and Cheese   Oven Setting 350°F, Mark 4

1 *thick slice of ham or bacon* per person   *Cheese Foundation*
tin of tomatoes

Place the ham in the bottom of an oven dish and pour over it the tinned tomatoes. Cover with Cheese Foundation and bake in a pre-heated oven until the ham is tender (about 30 minutes). Serve hot.

Chicory and Ham au Gratin   Oven Setting 375°F, Mark 5

To serve 4 allow:

2 *heads of chicory*
4 *thin slices of ham*
8 *tablespoons Cheese Foundation*
2 *tablespoons top milk*

½ *teaspoon lemon juice, fresh or bottled*
breadcrumbs
a little grated cheese – parmesan if
  possible
½ *oz butter or margarine*

Simmer chicory until tender. Strain and dry. Slice each head in half lengthwise. Wrap each piece in a slice of ham and place in a greased oven dish.

Measure Cheese Foundation into a small pan and place over very gentle heat. Add lemon to the top milk and stir into the warm Foundation with a wooden spoon. Pour mixture over the chicory. Cover with crumbs and cheese, and dot with margarine.

Cook in pre-heated oven for 20 minutes. If necessary, brown under the grill for a further few minutes.

Cauliflower au Gratin   Oven Setting 425°F, Mark 7

Allow:

a cauliflower, white and close	*brown breadcrumbs*
Cheese Sauce 1 (*p.* 7),	*a little grated cheese*
enough to cover cauliflower	

Cut away the outer leaves and tie the cauliflower in a thin cloth. Plunge it, head downward, into a pan of fast-boiling slightly salted water – enough water to cover the vegetable. Place lid on pan and boil until the cauliflower is tender without being too soft. Lift it carefully, still in its cloth, and perch on the rim of a pudding basin to drain.

Then turn the cauliflower on to a serving oven dish, cover with plenty of Cheese Sauce, and top with crumbs and cheese.

Brown for 15–20 minutes in a pre-heated oven.

Cauliflower au Gratin can also be made with *Cheese Sauce* 2 (p. 85).

Leek au Fromage

To serve 4 allow:

1½ lbs leeks	*salt and pepper*
1 oz butter	*4–5 tablespoons Cheese Foundation*
2 tablespoons olive oil	

Trim the outer leaves, most of the top and the base from each leek. Slice down the centre, open out and clean well under cold water. Cut into small pieces about ¼ inch thick.

Heat the butter and oil in a saucepan and add the leeks and seasoning. Cover and simmer gently for about 15 minutes or until the leeks are tender. Transfer to a shallow dish, cover with Cheese Foundation and place in the oven or under the grill for the cheese to warm through and brown.

Stuffed Baked Potatoes   Oven Setting 375°F, Mark 5

For each serving allow:

> 1 *well scrubbed potato*   2 *tablespoons Cheese Foundation*
> *melted butter or olive oil*   *salt and pepper to taste*

Prick potatoes with a fork, then brush with the melted butter or oil. Place in the centre of the pre-heated oven and bake for 1½–2 hours (or until the potatoes feel tender when gently pressed).

Cut in half lengthwise, scoop out insides into a bowl and mix with the Cheese Foundation. Add salt and pepper to taste, then return the mixture to the potato skins and place under the grill for a few minutes to reheat and brown.

This, served with a poached egg on top, makes a delicious supper dish.

Cheese Foundation is also used in the following recipes:

Cheese Pancakes p. 26.
Cheese Spreads pp. 68, 69, 70.
Egg and Cheese Filling p. 69.
Egg Vol-au-Vents p. 49.
Ham and Cheese Filling p. 69.
Ham and Cheese Rolls p. 19.
Potato au Gratin p. 124.
Potato and Cheese Volcanoes p. 118.
Savoury Apple Rings p. 20.
Savoury Bread Slices p. 20.
Tuna Fish and Cheese Filling p. 61.
Tuna Fish and Cheese Fritters p. 19.

BATTER MIX

BATTER MIX is made in a matter of moments, but, in an airtight container, will keep more or less indefinitely. Once you have this mix at your disposal, fritters, pancakes and drop scones, in all their varieties, are quickly and easily prepared. The batter can be cooked as soon as it is made – no leaving to stand for an hour or more as advised in most orthodox batter recipes.

Batter Mix

Sieve together and store:

> 1 *lb plain flour*
> 2½ *teaspoons bicarbonate of soda*
> 5 *teaspoons cream of tartar*

Batter Mix Recipes

Coating Batter

SMALL QUANTITY	MEDIUM QUANTITY	LARGE QUANTITY
5 *fluid oz Batter Mix*	6½ *fluid oz Batter Mix*	8 *fluid oz Batter Mix*
suitable seasoning	*suitable seasoning*	*suitable seasoning*
1 *small egg and liquid together to amount to 4 fluid oz*	1 *medium egg and liquid together to amount to 5 fluid oz*	1 *large egg and liquid together to amount to 6 fluid oz*

Empty the measured Batter Mix into a basin and add the seasoning.

SEASONING FOR A FISH BATTER OR SAVOURY FRITTERS

Salt and pepper and when suitable any of the following:
mustard   curry powder   celery salt   garlic salt or powder.

SEASONING FOR SWEET FRITTERS

sugar and, when suitable, *spices.*

Break the egg into the measure and add to this the liquid – enough so that the egg and liquid together amount to the correct number of fluid ounces. Any liquid can be used that harmonizes with the food to be coated. Thin liquids make lighter batters. Milk alone is too heavy, so when used by itself, it should be diluted with water. Here is a selection of liquids from which to choose.

A CHOICE OF LIQUIDS FOR A FISH BATTER OR SAVOURY FRITTERS

Stock milk water beer cider wine lemon juice tomato juice commercial sauces and ketchups 1 *tablespoon olive oil* (this is good in fish batters).

A CHOICE OF LIQUIDS FOR SWEET FRITTERS

milk water fruit juices and squashes syrups sweet sherry wine or cider

Slowly add the egg and liquid from the measure to the mix in the basin, beating it in with a fork until the ingredients are well blended. Continue to beat the mixture for about a minute. Turn the batter, or some of it, into a pie dish to make the coating process easier. Dip the food to be coated, and when completely covered, lift it with a kitchamajig or a perforated spoon and allow to drain before sliding it into a frying pan with plenty of hot lard, good cooking fat, butter* or oil. When the underside is brown, if any of the batter has rolled off the sides, fold this back on to the fish or fritter before turning it over. Fritters can also be deep fried.

When both sides are brown and crisp, drain on absorbent paper. Serve as quickly as possible, or keep, for a short while only, in a medium hot oven.

Any surplus batter, if covered and stored in a refrigerator, will keep for some days. It may turn an odd colour, but is easily revived by the addition of a little more Batter Mix and a good beat with a fork. Those with no refrigerator will unfortunately have to use all their prepared coating batter on the day it is made.

SURPLUS SAVOURY COATING BATTER

This coating batter, when fried on its own, makes nice little fritters, good to serve with most grilled or fried savoury dishes, especially so

---

* When frying with butter, add a teaspoon of olive or salad oil to prevent burning.

with eggs and bacon. When only a very small quantity is available, this can be used in *Battered Potato Slices* (p. 118).

FRITTERS

These are certainly the busy housewife's friend, not only for the ease and speed of their preparation, but because they can be made either of foods fully or partially cooked, or raw foods that will cook quickly. The only proviso is that the food used must be firm enough not to disintegrate when dipped in the coating batter.

BATTER-COATED FISH, AND SAVOURY FRITTERS

Fish Fillets and Steaks, Scampi and Prawns

These are all good when fried in a coating batter (pp. 17–18) in which the egg has been mixed with *milk, water, anchovy essence and* 1 *tablespoon olive oil.*

Sardine Fritters

Strain the *sardines* over the egg in the measure and include the *sardine oil* in the coating batter liquid. Dip each sardine individually and fry (pp. 17–18).

Tuna Fish and Cheese Fritters

Strain *the liquor of a tin of tuna fish* over the egg in the measure and include it in the coating batter liquid. Mash the fish with a fork and add enough *Cheese Foundation* (p. 7) to form the mixture into cakes. Dip and fry (pp. 17–18).

Sliced Meat Fritters

These are a good way of using *cold joints or tinned meats.* Cut the meat into fairly thin slices – allowing two for each fritter. Sandwich each pair with a choice of *chutney, horseradish sauces* 1 *or* 2 (pp. 77, 87), or *mustard.* Dip and fry (pp. 17–18).

Ham and Cheese Rolls

Spread *thin slices of cooked ham* with either *Cheese Foundation* (p. 7) or *Cream Cheese* (p. 110). Roll these up and fasten them with wooden cocktail sticks. Dip and fry (pp. 17–18). Remove cocktail sticks before serving.

Ham and Banana Fritters

Roll 1 *or* 2 *thin slices of lean ham* round *each banana*, if necessary fasten them with cocktail sticks. Dip and fry (pp. 17–18), not too quickly as the banana must be given time to heat right through.

Frankfurter Fritters

Frankfurters fried in a tasty coating batter make an excellent hot luncheon or supper dish.

Cheese Fritters

These are a good way of using up a *Cheddar type cheese* when it is getting dry.
    Cut cheese into ¼ inch slices. Add *dry mustard* to the *Batter Mix*. The fritters are improved when *beer* is included in the coating batter liquid (pp. 17–18).

Savoury Apple Rings

Peel and core *cooking apples* and slice into rings. Divide these into pairs and sandwich together with a choice of *chutney, Cheese Foundation* (p. 7) or *Cream Cheese* (p. 110). Either of the cheese fillings can be mixed with a choice of *minced ham, finely chopped celery or green peppers.* Dip and fry (p. 178).

Savoury Bread Slices

Cut *slices of brown bread,* allowing two for each fritter. Sandwich these with *the same cheese fillings given for savoury apple rings.* Dip and fry (pp. 17–18).

Onion Rings

These are delicious, a universal favourite, and especially appreciated with mixed grills, steaks, chops, liver, sausage and bacon.
    Cut the *onions* into thin slices, and push the rings out with your thumbs. Dip and fry the rings individually (pp. 17–18).

Vegetable Fritters

Vegetables such as *sprouts, cauliflower, celery, leeks* and *vegetable marrow* are all good in fritter form. They provide a change, make a little go a long way, and are a good way of using up left-overs.

When preparing fresh vegetables for fritters, they must first be partially cooked, preferably pressure cooked or steamed. Before cooking, divide cauliflower into flowerettes, cut celery and leeks into 2-inch lengths and marrow into ½-inch rings.

When using a pressure cooker, cook for about 2 minutes at 15 lb pressure over 2½ fluid oz salted water, and strain the vegetables over the egg in the measure so that the liquor can be included in the coating batter. When the vegetables are steamed or boiled, or when leftover vegetables are used, see that these are as dry as possible before they are dipped in the coating batter and fried (pp. 17–18).

Potato Fritters (p. 118).

Sweet Corn Fritters

These fritters are made with Batter Mix but not dipped in coating batter. They are delicious served with meat, poultry, fish, bacon, sausages, eggs or on their own dredged with grated cheese or served with a savoury sauce.

To serve 4–6 allow:

> *a 15–16 oz tin of sweet corn,*   *Batter Mix, enough to make the*
> *cream style*   *mixture the consistency of a*
> *1 egg*   *fruit cake batter*
> *salt and pepper to taste*

Mix the ingredients and beat well with a fork. Drop spoonfuls of the mixture into a pan of hot fat, and flatten these with a fish slice, and brown on both sides.

Uncooked sweet corn batter keeps well in the refrigerator. This is useful, as it can be used with other foods.

Filled Sweet Corn Fritters

To make these, a prepared *Sweet Corn Fritter Batter* is used in conjunction with any cooked, sausage-shaped foods such as:

> *frankfurters,*   *minced cooked meat, bound with*
> *cooked sausages,* *a choice of: creamed potatoes (p.* 115)*,*
> *elongated slices of meat* *Cheese Foundation or Cream Cheese*
> *or poultry,*   *(pp.* 7 *and* 110)

Drop large spoonfuls of the batter into hot fat. Flatten well to make thin rectangular fritters. Place a Frankfurter, or other chosen food, on top of each fritter. When the bottom begins to brown, turn up the sides round the filling, and press the edges together on top of filling. Turn fritters several times until brown and crisp all round and the food in the middle is hot.

NOTE: Should fillings be a little too moist for fritters, the addition of *fresh breadcrumbs* will rectify the trouble.

Additional savoury fritters can be made by frying the following mixtures, once they have been dipped in a coating batter:

Salmon and Tuna Fish Filling p. 63.
Cornish Pasty Filling p. 64.
Curry Filling p. 64.
Bacon and Egg Filling pp. 67–8.
Egg and Cheese Filling p. 69.
Ham and Cheese Filling p. 69.
Beurrek Filling pp. 68–9.
Croquette Mixtures pp. 92, 93, 94.
Creamed Potatoes p. 115.

SWEET FRITTERS

Apple Fritters

To make a change from plain apple fritters, prepare *the apples* as given for *Savoury Apple Rings,* but sandwich the rings together with a choice of *jam, thick honey, lemon curd, mince meat,* or *Butterscotch Sauce* (p. 80). *Sweet cider or white wine* are good mixed with the egg in the coating batter. Dredge the freshly fried fritters with *caster sugar and cinnamon* (optional).

 Serve, if liked, with *cream, custard,* or a *Hard Sauce* (pp. 105, 113 or 82).

Orange Fritters

Before peeling *the oranges,* grate off *some of the rind,* crush it well with *a little sugar* and add this to the dry *Batter Mix.* If, however, you are anxious to save time and have a jar of *Orange Flavouring* (p. 167), you can use that. Mix the egg for the *coating batter* with *orange juice or orange squash*. Cut each orange horizontally into 4 slices. Remove all the pips before dipping and frying (pp. 17–18).

These fritters are really delicious. They can be served with *heated Orange or Lemon 'Syrup* (pp. 82–3), *cream* or *custard*, or just dredged with *caster* or *icing sugar*.

Banana Fritters

After peeling, the *bananas* can be dipped whole in a well-flavoured coating batter, or split lengthwise and sandwiched together with *jam* before dipping and frying (pp. 17–18).

These can be served with *Vanilla Ice Cream* (p. 190) – the still cold, yet melting ice cream is delicious with the hot fritters.

Tinned Fruit Fritters

All hard tinned fruits make excellent fritters. Mix the egg for the coating batter with some of *the juice from the tin, diluted with a little water, sweet wine or cider*.

Pineapple Fritters

Of all tinned fruits, pineapple makes the best fritters.

Prepare the coating batter as given above. When using chunks or pieces, mix these with the batter, drop spoonfuls of the mixture into the hot fat, and flatten these out. When using rings, dip and fry each ring individually (p. 18).

Pineapple Fritters are delicious with *hot ham or bacon*. When making these, use *pineapple juice and ham stock* in the coating batter.

Bread and Jam or Lemon Curd Fritters

For each fritter allow:

2 *thinly cut slices of bread,*   *Sweet Coating Batter (pp. 17–18)*
    crusts removed
jam, lemon curd or Instant
    Lemon Curd (p. 71)

Spread jam or lemon curd on one slice of bread, cover with the second. Dip and fry (pp. 17–18).

Tipsy Fritters

These are made with:

sponge cakes   white wine   raspberry jam   Sweet coating batter* (pp. 17–18)

Slice the sponge cakes in half horizontally. Sprinkle the cut sides with white wine – enough to flavour well, but not to make the sponge cakes too soggy. Sandwich the soaked halves together again with a spreading of raspberry jam. Dip and fry (pp. 17–18).

These excellent fritters are good served with cream, ice cream or custard.

PANCAKES

These delicious light pancakes are allied to the fritter family, and the pancake batter, like the coating batter, is cooked as soon as it is prepared. But unlike the coating batter, the entire amount of pancake batter must be turned into pancakes and none of it stored for future use. It is the unwanted pancakes that can be stored – they will keep for some time – and then, when needed, can be resuscitated to be as good as when first made. Thus when the one batch of pancakes is to be served on more than one occasion, some may be given savoury fillings and others sweet. In that case, omit any seasoning when preparing the pancake batter.

Pancake Batter and How to Make Pancakes

5 *fluid oz Batter Mix*	1 *small egg and milk together*
½ *teaspoon salt and a little pepper*	*to amount to 5 fluid oz*
or 1 *dessertspoon sugar*	3 *fluid oz warm water*

Empty the measured Batter Mix into a basin and, when used, add seasoning.

Break the egg into the measure and add the milk. Beat well, add the water and beat again. Pour the mixture gradually into the Batter Mix, beating with a fork as you pour. After a final beat, strain the batter into a jug.

Use a small pan, not larger than 8 inches across, preferably an

---

* Include some white wine in the coating batter.

omelette pan which is never washed with water but cleaned with salt, or a non-stick frying pan. If you must use a water-washed pan and the pancakes stick, put plenty of salt in it, heat well and rub it out with absorbent paper or newspaper.

Heat the pan, and for the first pancake melt ¼ *oz butter* (subsequent pancakes will require considerably less). Pour a little of the batter into the sizzling butter, not quite enough to cover the bottom of the pan.

After a few seconds, when the underside is just beginning to set, tilt the pan this way and that, so that the top liquid rolls over the sides of the pancake and thus covers the rest of the pan. When the pancake surface begins to bubble, work round the edges with a knife, shake the pan gently, and turn the pancake over to cook the other side. A palette knife simplifies the operation.

As the pancakes are cooked, pile those to be served immediately, one on top of the other, on to a warm plate. Keep these warm, either on top of a saucepan of boiling water or in the coolest possible oven. They can now, if wished, be left for some while before filling and serving.

Place the pancakes to be stored on a wire cake tray to cool. When quite cold, stack on top of each other, wrap in 'Look', then store in the refrigerator. We find that stored like this, they keep perfectly fresh for at least a week.

Without a refrigerator, they keep 3 to 4 days in an airtight tin.

How to Reheat Pancakes

When Stuffed. Place hot filling in the centre of each pancake, roll up, arrange in an oven dish and cover with 'Look'.

Warm through, either in the coolest position of a cool oven for as long as you want, or if you are in a hurry, at the top of a hot oven for a few minutes.

Plain. These can be reheated in the following ways:

1. In a sauce.

2. Stacked on top of each other between two plates over a saucepan of boiling water.

3. Fried ½ minute per side in a frying pan lightly brushed with butter.

When it comes to pancake fillings, the choice must be unlimited. Cook books, daily papers and magazines all offer suggestions, many of them mouth-watering. Here are some of our choosing.

C.A.—B

SAVOURY PANCAKES

Sausage Pancakes and Apple Sauce

Allow:

> as many sausages as pancakes
> Apple Purée (pp. 132–3)

Prick the sausages and place them in a frying pan with a little boiling water. Cook for a few minutes, turning frequently, until the water has evaporated. Brown them in the dry pan for about 10 minutes. Roll each sausage in a hot pancake and serve with hot Apple Purée.

Cheese Pancakes

Allow *for each pancake:*

> 1 *tablespoon Cheese Foundation (p. 7)*
> 1 *teaspoon grated parmesan or*
> 1 *dessertspoon grated Cheddar Cheese*

Spread the hot pancakes with the Cheese Foundation. Roll them up. Place them in a grill pan. Sprinkle with the cheese and brown under the grill. Serve immediately.

Asparagus Pancakes

To serve 4 allow:

> 12 *oz tin asparagus spears*   *salt and pepper to taste*
> 2 *tablespoons Basic Cream*   *4 pancakes*
>   *Sauce (p. 84)*
> 2 *tablespoons asparagus liquid*

Strain the asparagus over a basin. Heat the Cream Sauce in a saucepan, stir in the liquid and gently fold in the asparagus. Add salt and pepper if necessary.

Fill 4 pancakes with the mixture and roll up Arrange in an oven dish, cover with Look, and place in the oven (See reheating, p. 25).

This makes a good starter to a dinner party.

Savoury Gateau Pancake

To serve 4 allow:

> 8 *pancakes*   *about 1 pint Cheese Sauce 1 or 2 (pp. 7 and 85)*
>   *or Curry Sauce (p. 85)*
>   *or Tomato Sauce (p. 85)*

If the pancakes have been stored, reheat over a saucepan of boiling water.

To make the gateau, place a pancake flat on a heatproof dish and spread with the chosen sauce. Cover with a second pancake and more sauce. Repeat until all the pancakes have been used. Cover the whole gateau with the remaining sauce. Serve immediately or keep warm in a slow oven.

NOTE. A little diced cooked sea food or poultry can be added to the sauce.

Shell Fish Pancakes (*see Filling*, p. 61)

Fish Cream Pancakes (*see Filling*, p. 62)

Tuna Fish and Cheese Pancakes (*see Filling*, p. 61)

Mushroom and Mushroom and Egg Pancakes (*see Filling*, p. 67)

Kidney Pancakes (*see Filling*, p. 66)

Liver and Bacon Pancakes (*see Filling*, p. 66)

Game, Poultry and Meat Pancakes (*see Filling*, p. 65)

Bacon Pancakes (p. 31)

Beef Pancakes (p. 31)

SWEET PANCAKES

Pancakes in a Lemon and Orange Sauce

To serve 4 allow:

8 *pancakes*	3 *tablespoons orange juice*
1 *oz butter*	1 *tablespoon lemon juice*
2 *oz caster sugar*	

Melt the butter in a large frying pan, add the sugar and fruit juices. Simmer gently until the sugar is dissolved, stirring continuously to prevent burning.

Fold pancakes and place in the pan. Spoon over some of the sauce to warm them through and then place on a serving dish. Any sauce remaining in the pan should be poured over the pancakes before serving.

Banana and Fruit Sauce Pancakes

To serve 4 allow:

8 *pancakes*	3 *tablespoons orange juice*
1 *oz butter*	1 *tablespoon lemon juice*
2 *oz caster sugar*	4 *bananas*

Melt the butter in a large frying pan, add the sugar and fruit juices. Simmer gently until the sugar is dissolved, stirring continuously to prevent burning.

Cut each banana in half lengthwise and place in the pan for a moment to warm through. Lie each half on a pancake and roll up.

Place in an oven dish. Cover with Look and warm through in a slow oven. Just before serving, reheat the sauce and pour over the pancakes.

Butterscotch Pancakes

Butterscotch Sauces and Fillings (pp. 80–1 and 73) are all good in or over pancakes.

Lemon Curd Pancakes

Spread hot *lemon curd* or *Instant Lemon Curd* (p. 71) either on the hot pancakes or before they are reheated.

Apple Pancakes

Fill pancakes with a choice of:

Apple Purée (*pp.* 132–3)	*any of the Apple Purée Fillings*
Apple Compôte (*p.* 134)	(*pp.* 72–3)

Pancakes with Hard Sauce or Rum Butter

Any of the *Hard Sauces* or *Rum Butter* (p. 82), are delicious with pancakes. These can either be served separately or spread on the hot pancakes immediately before serving.

Pancakes with Fruit Syrups

Serve the hot pancakes with any of the *Fruit Syrups* (pp. 82–3). The syrup must also be hot.

Crêpes Suzette

To serve 4 allow:

8 *pancakes*	½ *teaspoon grated orange rind*
1 *oz butter*	½ *teaspoon grated lemon rind*
1 *oz caster sugar*	4 *tablespoons Cointreau, Curacao or*
juice of 1 *orange*	*Grand Marnier*
	2 *tablespoons brandy*

Fold pancakes in four.

Melt the butter in a frying pan. Add sugar, orange juice, rind and liqueur. Bring to the boil.

Add pancakes, heat through, turning twice. Transfer to serving dish, pour over brandy, set alight and serve immediately.

Pancake Gateau

To serve 4 allow:

8 *pancakes*	*apricot jam or lemon curd*	*icing sugar*

If the pancakes have been stored, reheat over a saucepan of boiling water.

To make the gateau, place a pancake flat on a heatproof dish and spread it with a little warm jam or lemon curd. Cover with a second pancake and more jam or curd. Repeat until all the pancakes have been used.

Keep warm covered with a basin in a very cool oven.

Immediately before serving dust the top pancake with a little icing sugar.

DROP SCONES

Drop Scones, otherwise Girdle Scones or Scotch Pancakes, sweet or savoury, are always popular. With Batter Mix they are quick and easy to make on a girdle, a heavy frying pan, or an electric hot plate. To grease the cooking surface, whichever it is, rub over with a small lump of butcher's suet, tied up in a piece of cloth. When stored in the refrigerator for this purpose, the suet will keep for many months. Do not make too large a quantity of drop scone batter, as it must be transformed into drop scones as soon as it is prepared, and these are so much nicer eaten fresh.

Sweet Drop Scone Batter

SMALL QUANTITY	MEDIUM QUANTITY	LARGE QUANTITY
5 *fluid oz Batter Mix*	7½ *fluid oz Batter Mix*	½ *pint Batter Mix*
1 *dessertspoon sugar*	3 *teaspoons sugar*	1 *tablespoon sugar*
1 *small egg and milk together amounting to 4 fluid oz*	1 *medium egg and milk together amounting to 6 fluid oz*	1 *large egg and milk together amounting to 8 fluid oz*

Savoury Drop Scone Batter

SMALL QUANTITY	MEDIUM QUANTITY	LARGE QUANTITY
5 *fluid oz Batter Mix*	7½ *fluid oz Batter Mix*	½ *pint Batter Mix*
salt and pepper to taste	*salt and pepper to taste*	*salt and pepper to taste*
1 *dessertspoon parmesan, finely grated*	3 *teaspoons parmesan, finely grated*	1 *tablespoon parmesan, finely grated*
1 *small egg and milk with a little tomato ketchup and Worcester sauce together amounting to 4 fluid oz*	1 *medium egg and milk with a little tomato ketchup and Worcester sauce together amounting to 6 fluid oz*	1 *large egg and milk with a little tomato ketchup and Worcester sauce together amounting to 8 fluid oz*

How to Prepare and Cook Drop Scone Batters

Empty the measured Batter Mix into a basin. Add the sugar or seasoning, and to a savoury batter, the cheese. Break the egg into the measure and add the liquid. Beat well and pour this gradually into the Batter Mix, beating with a fork as you pour.

While preparing the batter, heat the cooking surface. To test the temperature, drop a little of the mixture from a teaspoon on to the hot surface previously rubbed with the cloth-covered suet. If the sample bubbles and browns on the underside in one minute, the heat is correct.

Give the batter a final good beating. (For convenience, and to save making a mess, it is as well to have a large plate as close to the cooking surface as possible. This plate should be large enough to accommodate the basin of batter, the suet, the required spoons and a palette or pliable knife or a slice, for turning the scones.)

Drop the batter from a dessert- or tablespoon on to the hot surface (a teaspoon can be used for canapés). As soon as the scones begin to bubble, lift them with the knife or slice and replace them brown side up. Always rub the cooking surface again with the suet before dropping on fresh drop scones, and, if necessary, before replacing them after turning. When they are a golden brown on both sides and the batter in the middle is set, the scones are done. Lift them and slip them on top of each other into a folded tea towel. Leave them in this towel until they are wanted.

Just before serving, spread with *butter, cheese, or Savoury Spreads* (See **Index** under *Spreads*).

Bacon Pancakes

This extremely nice luncheon or supper dish – and especially so with a poached egg on top – is made with:

Rashers of fairly fat bacon and Savoury Drop Scone Batter (*p.* 30)

These, like drop scones, can be made on a girdle, an electric hot plate, or in a heavy frying pan. There is no need to grease the cooking surface.

Cut the bacon into pieces about ¾ inch by ¼ inch. Place these in clusters on the well-heated surface. Turn them now and again, until they are crisp and have exuded plenty of fat.

Pour over each cluster of cooked bacon a little of the prepared batter. When the mixture begins to bubble, turn the pancakes and brown the other side. Serve hot.

Beef Pancakes

To serve 4 allow:

4 *oz Batter Mix*	1 *small onion, finely chopped*
1 *egg*	4 *oz cooked minced beef*
¾ *pint milk and water*	*seasoning to taste*
lard	*butter*
	chopped parsley

Make a batter by breaking an egg into the Batter Mix, then beating in the milk and water slowly.

Heat some of the lard in a saucepan, and fry the onion until soft, then add minced beef and seasoning. Mix well together before stirring it into the batter.

Grease a hot frying pan with lard. Pour in enough of the batter thinly to cover the bottom of the pan. Cook quickly until crisp and brown on the underside, then turn and cook the other.

Place on a serving dish; spread with a little butter, sprinkle with chopped parsley, roll tightly, and keep hot until the rest of the pancakes are cooked. Serve.

PASTRY

THERE are probably more fallacies connected with pastry making than with any other branch of cooking. Of course good pastry requires some skill, but success depends on know-how and not on so-called light hands. Anyone who uses the right ingredients and sets about the job in the right way can be sure of producing the best possible pastry.

These days commercially-made doughs are very popular. Some are good, but all are far more costly and certainly no better than the doughs you can make yourself. Home-made doughs take only a few minutes to prepare and, unlike the bought ones, keep two to three weeks in a refrigerator, ready to be used as and how they are needed. Stored doughs should be wrapped in greaseproof paper.

DOUGHS

Pastry Doughs That Keep

Short Crust   Oven Setting 400°F, Mark 6

A nice, crumbly short crust is always welcome: and when you can make it easily without messing your hands, what could be better? That is exactly what can be done when using the Boiling Water Method.

It is made with:

> ½ *lb cooking fat* (any quality)   4 *fluid oz boiling water*
> 11 *oz self-raising flour*

This is the method:

Cut the fat into about six pieces and place in a mixing bowl. If cold and very hard, heat slightly or leave at room temperature for a while.

Pour the boiling water over the fat and stir energetically with a wooden spoon or kitchamajig and, at the same time, press the fat against the sides of the bowl until the fat and water have fused into a creamy mixture.

Sift the flour into the bowl and work it into the fat and water with a palette or flexible knife.

At this stage, if possible leave the bowl in a refrigerator or cool place for a short time, or, if more convenient, for several hours, so that the dough can harden enough for easy handling. Then dredge with flour, and knead well with floured hands, until you have a good, soft, pliable dough. All this can be done in the mixing bowl. Now the dough, or part of it, can be rolled out and baked immediately, or, when wrapped in grease-proof paper, or slipped into an empty flour bag, will keep for some time to be used as wanted. If left in a refrigerator for any length of time, the dough, especially when made of cheaper fat, may become too hard to manage with ease. This can be remedied by taking the dough out of the refrigerator before it is needed and working it once more with the hands before rolling it out.

Always bake in pre-heated oven

NOTE. A good sweet short crust pastry can be made with *Cake Foundation*. This is given on pp. 176, 177.

ROUGH PUFF AND PUFF PASTRIES

The secret of good flaky and puff pastries is certainly not the lightness of the cook's hand – the doughs thrive on rough treatment. Success depends on temperature and the ability to form the dough into layers of flour and water, fat and air. Bear this in mind when following the given directions and you can't go wrong.

Rough Puff Dough Oven Setting 450°F, Mark 8

This satisfactory flaky pastry can be made all the year round without a refrigerator.

It is made with:

> *a good quality cooking fat* (any weight from ¼ lb to 1 lb)
> *plain flour* (double the chosen weight of fat)
> *a pinch of salt*
> *cold water*, as little as possible.

The smallest quantity to handle easily is: *¼ lb fat and ½ lb flour*, and the largest: 1 *lb fat and* 2 *lbs flour*.

The fat must be cold and hard, therefore in hot weather, those without a refrigerator should harden the fat in cold water before starting the operation.

1. Sift the flour with a pinch of salt into a large mixing bowl.
2. Cut the fat into the flour, in pieces of roughly 1 oz.
3. With one hand, dribble cold water, from a cup or small jug, all

round the inside rim of the bowl. With the other hand, rotate a fork in the mixture in small circles, working in the water, and at the same time forming the dough into rough-looking sections. Use as little water as possible, so that the dough will not become too moist. Experience will soon show just how much is needed.

4. With your hands, mould the sections into one lump.

5. Place the dough on to a well floured working surface or pastry board.

6. Here the rough treatment is necessary, and for this you need an old-fashioned wooden rolling pin with easily gripped handles, not knobs. Raise the pin well above your shoulder and bang it down – crash, wallop – on top of the dough until it is flattened out. (This is a grand outlet for pent-up emotions. Try it.)

7. Now using the rolling pin in the conventional way, roll the dough into an oblong about $\frac{1}{4}$ inch thick.

8. Make it into a kind of envelope, by folding the front third over the centre third, and the back third over them both. Press the open edges to contain the air. Turn the dough to the left, leaving the closed side on the right.

9. Rib and roll alternately, until the dough is once more an oblong. (Ribbing is pressing the rolling pin down on the dough at regular intervals, making a switch-back effect.)

10 to 19. Repeat 8 and 9 five times.

20. Repeat 8 once.

The dough can now be used, or when wrapped in greaseproof paper or put in an empty flour bag will keep up to two weeks in a refrigerator and up to a week in any really cool place.

If possible, chill prepared dishes for a short while before putting them in the *pre-heated oven*.

Puff Pastry Dough   Oven Setting 475°F, Mark 9

Though puff pastry is considered one of the highest cooking achievements, there is no cook, with a refrigerator and a reliable oven, who cannot produce it to perfection with very little trouble. Unfortunately it is only in very cold weather that puff pastry can be made by those with no refrigerator.

It is made with:

> *equal quantities of plain flour and fat*
> *a pinch of salt and very little icy cold water*

The fat must consist of:

> 1 *part butter or a good margarine*
> 3 *parts English or Danish lard* (never use Ameri-
> can, as it is much too soft)

The smallest quantities to manage easily are:

> ½ *lb plain flour*   2 *oz butter*   6 *oz lard*

The largest recommended quantities are:

> 1½ *lbs plain flour*   6 *oz butter*   1 *lb* 2 *oz lard*

Leave the lard in the refrigerator until the moment it is needed.

1. Sift the flour and salt into a large mixing bowl.
2. Cut or grate the butter or margarine into it.
3. Rub this fat into the flour, using thumbs and finger tips to start with, then the palms of your hands, and at the same time lifting the mixture and showering it back into the bowl. This helps to aerate.
4. With one hand, dribble icy cold water, from a cup or small jug, all round the inside rim of the bowl. With the other hand, rotate a fork in the mixture in small circles, working in the water, and at the same time forming the dough into rough-looking sections. The dough must be pliable yet not too moist. Experience will soon show how much water is needed; the correct amount is important.
5. With your hands, mould the sections into one lump.
6. Place the dough on to a well floured working surface or pastry board.
7. Knead the dough for about two minutes.
8. Roll it out to a thickness of about ¼ inch.
9. Lay the lard, straight out of the refrigerator, or equally cold and hard, on the dough.
10. Fold the dough round the lard, pressing the edges firmly together to ensure that the lard is completely covered.
11 to 25. These stages are the same as 6 to 20 given for rough puff dough (p. 35). But should you be unfortunate and find the fat oozing out of the dough, either because your lard was not cold enough, or your kitchen too hot, stop the operation, store the dough as it is in the refrigerator, and carry out the omitted rolls, folds and turns on the whole lump of dough, before the first portion is used.

Wrap the dough in greaseproof paper or put in an empty flour bag and store in the refrigerator or an icy winter larder. Do not use till the next day. It will keep quite well for up to a fortnight, though vol-au-vent cases, vol-au-vent flans and pastry slices (pp. 41–2) should be baked within two to three days. However, once they are baked, these keep in tins for many months. Of course the older dough can be used for tarts, pasties, turnovers, fried pies and pastry cases of different shapes and sizes. These will not rise to the same heights as the vol-au-vents, but will be nice, rich and flaky. When the dough is older than a week, give the chunk about to be used a few preliminary rolls, folds and turns.

To get the best out of your puff pastry, switch on your oven 475°F, Mark 9, before you take the dough out of the refrigerator. Also, once the dough has been fashioned, put it back in the refrigerator for a short spell, to *ensure that icy cold dough goes into the very hot oven*. To guarantee that your vol-au-vent cases and puff slices do indeed 'fly in the wind', they must enter the oven placed directly on a very cold baking sheet.

Fleur and Almond Cinnamon Pastries

These doughs must be prepared, rolled out, fashioned and baked all at the one session. However, when stored in airtight containers, the resulting delicious, rich, short pastry tartlet and flan cases will keep fresh for many months.

Sweet Fleur Pastry   Oven Setting 400°F, Mark 6

> 12 *oz plain flour and a pinch of salt*   4 *oz caster sugar*
> 7 *oz butter or margarine*   2 *egg yolks*

Sift the flour and salt into a large mixing bowl. Rub in the fat and then add the sugar and egg yolks. Work the mixture with your hands and knead it well until it is soft and very pliable. Of course, the same result can be achieved with the help of an electric blender. Now roll the dough $\frac{1}{16}$ to $\frac{1}{10}$ of an inch and fashion into cases as explained on pp. 39–40. Bake about 15 minutes in pre-heated oven.

These tartlet and flan cases, when kept in airtight tins, literally remain oven-fresh for months on end. Nevertheless, should you have doubts as to their crispness, a short spell on a wire tray in a cool oven ensures a further satisfactory lengthy spell back in their tin. Thus with fleur cases in your cupboard, a selection of sweet fillings (see **Index**) and a supply of your own cream (pp. 104–105), a delicious sweet is always to hand. . .

Savoury Fleur Pastry   Oven Setting 400°F, Mark 6

This makes excellent cases for savoury fillings, just the thing for parties and receptions. These do not keep as long in tins as the sweet fleur-cases, but can easily be made a week or more before they are wanted. If savoury cases are needed for long keeping, these can be made by omitting the cheese and increasing the flour a little – sufficient to make the dough easy to handle. The flavour will not be as good, but they will then keep as long in tins as their sweet counterparts.

12 *oz plain flour*	*a pinch of cayenne*
1 *teaspoon salt*	7 *oz butter or margarine*
1 *teaspoon dry mustard*	2 *oz finely grated parmesan cheese*
¼ *teaspoon pepper*	2 *egg yolks*

Sift the flour and seasoning into a large mixing bowl. Rub in the fat and cheese. Add the egg yolks and work the mixture with your hands and knead it well until it is soft and pliable. These directions can also be carried out with an electric blender. Now roll dough $\frac{1}{16}$ to $\frac{1}{10}$ of an inch and fashion into cases, as explained on pp. 39–40. Bake about 15 minutes in pre-heated oven.

For choice of fillings, see pp. 61–64 and 69.

Almond Cinnamon Pastry   Oven Setting 350°F, Mark 4

This is a special pastry of Danish origin – not cheap, but excellent for parties.

5½ *oz plain flour*	5½ *oz ground almonds*
½–1 *level teaspoon cinnamon*	4 *oz butter or margarine*
5½ *oz caster sugar*	

Sift the flour and cinnamon into a large mixing bowl. Add the sugar and almonds. Cut the fat into the other ingredients and work all of them together, by hand or mechanically, until a paste is formed. Knead well, roll out, and fashion into cases as described on pp. 39–40.

Bake in pre-heated oven for about 15 minutes, or until golden brown.

PASTRY CASES

Many pastry dishes are made by filling already baked pastry cases with savoury or sweet mixtures. It is invaluable to have a selection of these cases always available, and time devoted to making them is surely well spent. Stored in airtight tins, cases made with Short Crust and Rough

Puff doughs (pp. 33–35) will keep for some weeks. Vol-au-Vents and other cases made from Puff Pastry dough (pp. 35–37) and Almond Cinnamon dough (p. 38) keep for months. Cases made from Fleur Pastry (p. 37) keep the longest of all.

Fleur and Almond Cinnamon cases are always served cold with cold fillings.

Cases made from Short, Rough Puff or Puff doughs that have been stored for some time, whether the filling is to be hot or cold, will be better for a spell in the oven to regain their original freshness, either just before receiving their hot fillings or early enough to get quite cold again if the filling is to be cold. Place the cases on a wire cake tray and either put them in a very hot oven, with the door slightly ajar, for about 5 to 10 minutes, or in the coolest possible oven for an hour or so.

When fillings contain raw eggs the procedure is different—see appropriate recipes.

Other savoury and sweet fillings are given on pp. 61–75.

Flan and Tartlet Cases

Made with Short Crust, Rough Puff, Puff and Fleur Doughs

When dishes or tins are lined with dough, the sides are liable to collapse during the baking, unless propped up with crusts or beans. This can easily be avoided, by inverting the dish, tin or case, and moulding the dough over the outside.

Of course metal containers can be used, but we find those made of foil preferable; these are excellent in every way. Alcan makes dishes and cases in a variety of shapes and sizes. These are stocked at most large stores and supermarkets.

We consider the best way to make pastry cases is to fashion each from its individual piece of dough. The dough is rolled into balls when using Short Crust and Fleur Doughs, and cut into chunks when Rough Puff or Puff Doughs are used. This method may not be quicker, but it does ensure uniform thickness, and the pastry does not deteriorate from much handling, re-rolling, and the addition of extra flour. How thinly you roll your dough is a matter of taste, and experience will soon indicate the amount of dough needed for each ball or chunk to cover your particular dishes and cases. Roll the balls or chunks one by one on a piece of floured greaseproof paper (the dough is now easier to handle). Invert the tin, dish or case on top of the dough, which should be large enough to cut round the dish rim, leaving a margin of about $\frac{1}{8}$ inch.

When using Short Crust or Fleur Doughs, brush the containers with oil.

Lay the dough on top of the inverted dish and mould it gently but firmly round the sides. Place on a baking sheet and bake in pre-heated oven, correctly set for the dough used, for 10 to 15 minutes.

When baked a nice pale brown, take dishes out of the oven and place them, pastry side down, on a wire tray, which must not be too large for your oven. Carefully lever the containers out of the pastry, and return the cases on the wire tray to the oven for a few minutes to cook the insides. Cool and store.

Fillings are given on pp. 61–75. Also see Index under *Fillings*.

Flan and Tartlet Cases made with Almond Cinnamon Dough

Roll and cut the dough as given for Fleur Pastry, but this dough is too fragile to bake over an inverted tin or dish. Always use foil dishes for Almond Cinnamon Pastry, and line these with the dough.

Bake in pre-heated oven, 350°F, Mark 4, for about 15 minutes.

When baked, if necessary, remould into shape and leave for a few minutes to cool. Then invert on a wire tray. Gently press the bottom of the dish, and the case will be ejected without difficulty.

Fillings especially recommended for Almond Cinnamon Flans are:

Apple and Sherry (p. 72).
Butterscotch Nut (p. 73)
Cream Cheese and Kirsch (p. 111)
Rum Butter Filling (p. 73)

Cake Foundation Pastry Flans (p. 177)

VOL-AU-VENT CASES, PUFF PASTRY SLICES AND PASTRY HORNS

When you have a lump of good Puff Dough, not more than three days old, it is simple and amusing to make a supply of these cases for the future. They can be used in so many ways and on such varied occasions – for example, with rich and exotic fillings for parties, or with left-overs on hectic mid-week evenings, to masquerade as a special dish. A selection of fillings is given on pp. 61–75. Those for Baked Pastry Cases are suitable for vol-au-vents, unless stated otherwise. See also *Vol-au-Vents to the Rescue*, pp. 48–9.

Vol-au-Vent Cases

Large cases, suitable for fish, poultry or meat fillings, need:

> *about 3½ oz Puff Pastry Dough* (for each case)
> and *two pastry cutters, 4½ and 3½ inches*

Smaller cases need:

> *about 2 oz Puff Pastry* (for each case)
> and *two pastry cutters, 3½ and 2½ inches*

Minute cases just right for cocktail savouries or canapés need:

> *about ½ oz. Puff Pastry* (for each case)
> and *two pastry cutters, 2 and 1¼ inches*

Cut pieces of dough of the correct weight. Roll these, keeping them as circular as possible, until they are slightly bigger than the larger of the two cutters. Trim the circles with this cutter. Using the smaller cutter, cut out the centres. Set aside the outer rings. Roll out the centre rounds, again keeping them as circular as possible, until they are a little bigger than the larger cutter – how much does not seem to matter, but, to get a well shaped case, they must be definitely larger. Do not trim these rounds, just lay them on a cold baking sheet – never a hot or warm one. Brush round the edges with *a little cold water*. Fit the rings on to the rounds, leaving a little surround of dough.

If you want a glaze, brush with *egg, egg and milk, or just milk*. If you don't want the extra trouble, the vol-au-vents still look attractive when left unglazed.

Bake in a hot oven – 475°F, Mark 9 – for 10 minutes, and a little longer, if necessary, at a lower temperature.

If lids are needed for the cases, these are easily made from the scraps of dough left after the first cut. Knead these together, mould the lump into a rectangle and continue as for rough puff. Cut out small rounds and bake these with the cases.

Square Vol-au-Vent Cases

These are a novelty and so easy to make.

Roll out a piece of Puff dough to a square ¼ to ⅜ inch thick, according to its size. Cut the edges to true up the sides. Cut out a square in the centre, leaving a frame from ¼ to ⅜ inch wide, again according to the size of the square. Then continue as for the circular vol-au-vents.

Vol-au-Vent Flan Cases

These do look professional, and could not be more simple to make. Just follow the directions for Vol-au-Vent Cases, but instead of cutters of different sizes, use plates, and cut round these with a knife. Experience will soon show you how much dough is needed for the plates you have chosen. A really large flan can be made with a bread board and a large meat plate or a sandwich tin. The sandwich tin is a good idea if the flan is to be served with a jelly filling (pp. 74–5).

Puff Pastry Slices

These are the quickest of all the Puff Dough products, and stored in their tin, are ready to form the base of a number of good and equally speedy sweets.

Cut off a rectangular piece of fresh dough. Roll it to a thickness of $\frac{1}{4}$ to $\frac{3}{8}$ inch, keeping it symmetrical. Cut a fraction off each of the sides, and the resulting rectangle into oblongs or squares. Lay these on a cold baking sheet. Bake as for Vol-au-Vent Cases. See also p. 60.

Pastry Horns

For these you need the metal horns sold at most hardware stores, and the directions for making them are found on the boxes in which the metal horns are sold. The dough need not be very fresh, and re-rolled oddments can be used. These horns make attractive sweets, filled with *jam, lemon curd or ice cream, etc. See* pp. 71, 73, 190. Also, when very small horns are made, these are just right for cocktail savouries. *Suitable fillings are given on* pp. 61–70.

PASTRY DISHES

PIE-DISH PIES

Short and rough puff crusts are best for these – the moisture from the filling affects puff dough unfavourably. Use pie dishes with wide flat rims, to prevent the pastry falling in. Fill dish firmly to the brim. Crust holders can be used in deep dishes, but the food in the dish must be the main crust support. To get a nice thick edge without making extra strips of paste, roll the dough for the crust about an inch larger all round than the top of the dish. Moisten the rim with water. Lay the crust cover on it, and turn under the surplus dough. Press it down firmly, and at the same time decorate by alternately using your thumb and cutting with a knife. Make holes for ventilation.

Meat Pie-Dish Pies

Today it is agreed that casseroled meat should be cooked for a long time in a slow oven – perhaps not always as long and slowly as the Slow Cooking Method so strongly advocated in my other books – but certainly much more slowly than good short or flaky pastries demand. Cooking the raw meat under a dough lid is, to all intents and purposes, casseroling, and if the complete pie is cooked at one time in the same oven, neither the meat nor the pastry can be at their best.

The only way to get a satisfactory meat pie is to cook the meat first, early enough for it to get completely cold in the pie dish before the dough is applied. (Recipes for cooking these meats do not come within the scope of this book.) As soon as the meat is cooked, strain off the gravy or stock and pack the meat (cut into neat pieces) and any vegetables into a pie dish of the correct size.

When pies are to be served hot, add the gravy, if necessary thickened with *Manie Butter* (p. 78). Add sufficient to come near the top of the meat, but not cover it.

When pies are to be served cold with a gelatinous gravy, add only a few tablespoons of the hot stock and pour the remainder into a measure.

For both pies, chill the meat before applying the dough top, and in hot weather, with rough puff tops, chill again before baking. Timing and oven temperature must suit the type of dough used.

Meat pies to be eaten hot must be baked immediately before the meal.

Meat pies to be eaten cold must be baked well in advance of serving. Shortly before they come out of the oven, prepare the jelly. *For each ¼ pint of stock, allow 1 teaspoon powdered gelatine.* Soak this in a little cold water for 5 minutes. Meanwhile boil the stock and pour it over the soaked gelatine. Mix well. As soon as the pie comes out of the oven, place a funnel in the crust's hole, and pour in enough jelly to fill all the crevices and just come up to the pastry. Chill.

Fruit Pies

With soft fruit add no water, and only very little with hard fruit. As soft fruit shrinks considerably, use a shallow dish with a wide rim. Sprinkle a short crust top lavishly with caster sugar for the last 5 minutes of baking.

Pasties – Turnovers – Small Pies – Two Crust Tarts

These are most useful and adaptable, as they can be made with *Short* (pp. 33–4), *Rough Puff* (pp. 34–5) *or Puff* (pp. 35–7) *doughs*, filled with anything and everything, provided it is not too moist, is cooked, partially cooked or, if raw, will not take longer to cook than the pastry needs to become crisp and brown. They can be eaten hot or cold and can be made the day before, which makes them grand for picnics and packed lunches.

Pasties and Turnovers

These are made the same way, but with a savoury filling are known as 'pasties' and with a sweet filling as 'turnovers'.

Here is a quick and simple method of making them.

Cut off a piece of dough for each pasty or turnover. Roll these into approximate squares: don't worry to make them over-symmetrical or cut the edges, but roll puff dough thin, and rough puff and short doughs about $\frac{1}{8}$ inch thick. You will soon discover how much dough you need for the size of pasty required. Put the filling on to the front half of each square, leaving about $\frac{1}{2}$ inch of dough round the front and sides. Fold these dough edges over the filling. Brush them with a little water. Fold the uncovered dough over the filling on to the moistened edges. Press gently into position. Cut two ventilation slits. If you want a glaze, brush pasties *with egg, egg and milk, or milk only.*

Bake in pre-heated oven, short crust pasties 400°F, Mark 6; rough puff 450°F, Mark 8; and puff 475°F, Mark 9, until the pasties are nice and brown.

Small Pies

Cut off a piece of dough for each pie – about 3 oz. Halve each piece and roll the sections into rounds, as identical as you can get them without using a cutter. Roll puff dough very thin, and rough puff and short crust about $\frac{1}{8}$ inch thick. Place the filling on half the rounds, leaving about $\frac{1}{2}$ inch of uncovered dough round the filling. Moisten these sur-rounds with water. Top with the remaining rounds of dough. Press the edges together and then turn both the edges towards the centre. Press again to make a firm edge, first with your thumbs, then with the prongs of a fork. Cut ventilation slits in the centre in the form of a cross. Glaze and bake as given for pasties.

Small Pies can also be fried, see pp. 57–8.

Two Crust Tarts

These are made as given for *Covered Plate Tarts* (p. 50) and are just as suitable for savoury fillings as they are for sweet ones.

Fillings for Pasties, Turnovers, Small Pies and Two Crust Tarts

The choice must be more or less inexhaustible, and we can only suggest a few of the many:

SAVOURY FILLINGS

Salmon or Tuna Fish (p. 63)
Sardine (p. 63)
Cornish Pasty (p. 64)
Curry (p. 64)
Bacon and Egg (pp. 67–8)
Ham and Cheese (p. 69)
Egg and Cheese (p. 69)
Beurrek (pp. 68–9)
Croquette Mixtures (p. 68)

SWEET FILLINGS

Lemon Fillings (pp. 71–2)
Apple Purée Fillings (pp. 72–3)
Butterscotch Fillings (p. 73)

Tarts and Flans

These fall into two categories:

1. Already baked cases (pp. 38–42) are served with fillings: a, b, or c.

(a) The fillings are also cooked – a selection of these is given on pp. 61–73;

(b) they contain raw egg and are cooked in the baked cases;

(c) they are set in gelatine and are transferred to the baked cases just before serving (see pp. 74–5).

2. Uncooked fillings are baked in dough-lined flan tins or rings, or shallow metal or foil dishes.

The following Pastry Dishes come under 1(b) or 2.

SAVOURY TARTS AND FLANS

Quiche Lorraine 1   Oven Setting 400°F, Mark 6
To serve 4 allow:

6 *oz Short Crust Dough (pp.* 33–4)   ½ *pint plus* 1 *tablespoon milk*
4 *rashers bacon,* cut into small strips ½ *oz butter*
2 *teaspoons flour*   *salt and pepper*
½ *teaspoon mustard*   2 *eggs*
                                         Cayenne pepper

Line a well-greased, 8 inch sandwich tin with at least 1¼ inch sides, shallow, loose-bottomed cake tin, foil dish or flan ring with the dough. Fry the bacon lightly, then put it on the dough. Blend the flour and mustard with the tablespoon of milk. Heat, but do not boil, the half-pint milk, and add the butter and seasoning. Beat in the eggs. Pour this custard over the bacon. Sprinkle with a few grains of cayenne. Bake for 25–30 minutes in pre-heated oven. Serve hot or cold.

Quiche Lorraine 2   Oven Setting 375°F, Mark 5

To serve 2 allow:

  a 6 *inch Baked Pastry Case*   2½ *fluid oz milk*
  or two 4½ *inch Cases (pp.* 38–40)   *salt and pepper*
  2 *rashers bacon,* cut into small strips *a little grated cheese*
  1 *egg*

The baked case or cases can either be *Short Crust* (pp. 33–4), or if served cold, *Savoury Fleur pastry* (p. 38).

Fry the bacon lightly and put it in the case. Beat together the egg and milk. Season to taste and pour over the bacon. Sprinkle with the cheese. Bake in pre-heated oven until the custard has set – it must not boil. Serve hot or cold.

Cheese Tart   Oven Setting 400°F, Mark 6

To serve 4 allow:

  ¼ *lb Short Crust Dough (pp.* 33–4)   2 *egg yolks*
  4 *oz grated cheese* (preferably   3 *fluid oz creamy milk*
    Gruyère, Emmenthal or Jarlsberg)   *salt and pepper*
  2 *oz butter or margarine*

Roll out pastry thinly and line a deep 8 inch flan ring or sandwich tin (if too shallow, the filling will overflow). Put the cheese in a saucepan over very gentle heat, and with a wooden spoon blend it with the butter. Spread the mixture over the pastry base. Whisk the yolks into the milk, season and strain over the cheese spread. Bake until set in a pre-heated oven, about 20 minutes.

Serve hot or cold.

Cheese and Onion Tart   Oven Setting 400°F, Mark 6

To serve 4 allow:

8 oz Short Crust Dough (pp. 33–4) 5 oz grated cheese
2 eggs, well beaten   2 medium sized onions, finely chopped
     salt and pepper

Divide the dough into two, one piece a little larger. Roll them out so that the larger will line an 8 inch metal or foil dish, leaving a little extra pastry all round the rim, and the smaller is just right for the cover.

Mix the remaining ingredients. Blend well and transfer mixture to the lined dish. Put on the pastry lid and turn the spare pastry from the lining over on top of it. Press rim down with thumb and cut with a knife alternately.

Bake 30–45 minutes in a pre-heated oven.

Serve hot.

Cheese and Bacon Flan   Oven Setting 400°F, Mark 6

To serve 4 allow:

6 oz Short Crust Dough (pp. 33–4) 3 oz grated cheese
2 onions, finely sliced   2 eggs
¼ oz butter   8 fluid oz milk
3 rashers bacon, cut into pieces pinch of salt
   pinch of nutmeg

Line an 8 inch by, at least, 1¼ inch sandwich tin or flan ring with the dough. Fry the onions in a small saucepan with the butter, until a golden brown, having added the bacon as soon as the onions had clarified. Remove pan from heat and stir in half the cheese. Add the eggs, milk and seasoning, and pour the mixture into the flan. Sprinkle the rest of the cheese on top.

Bake in pre-heated oven for 30–40 minutes, or till brown.

Serve hot or cold.

Ham and Sweetcorn Flan   Oven Setting 375°F, Mark 5

To serve 4 allow:

8¾ *inch Baked Flan Case*   2 *eggs, beaten*
  (*short, rough puff or puff*)   *seasoning to taste*
  (*pp.* 33–40)   *brown crumbs*
15–16 *oz tin sweetcorn,*   *grated cheese* (*optional*)
  cream style   *a little butter or margarine*
4 *slices cooked ham, cut*
  in strips

Put the sweetcorn, ham and eggs into a basin, mix well, and season to taste. Transfer the mixture to the pastry case. Top with crumbs, a little cheese (if used) and dot with butter or margarine.

Bake in pre-heated oven until mixture has set and the top is nice and brown.

Serve hot or cold.

Ham and Egg Flans   Oven Setting 375°F, Mark 5

a large or several individual Baked   *Cheese Sauce* 1 *or* 2 (*pp.* 7 *and* 85)
  Pastry Cases, short crust, rough   or *Tomato Sauce* (*pp.* 85–6)
  puff or puff; savoury fleur (only   *brown crumbs*
  if served cold) (*pp.* 35–40)   *a little butter or margarine*
1 *slice cooked ham and* 1 *egg per*
  serving

Lay the ham on the bottom of the flans. Break eggs one by one into a cup and slip them carefully and symmetrically on top of the ham. Cover the eggs completely with the cheese sauce. Top with crumbs and dot with small dabs of butter or margarine.

Bake in pre-heated oven for about 20 minutes, or until eggs are set and the top is nice and brown.

Serve hot.

VOL-AU-VENTS TO THE RESCUE

Crises such as the arrival of unexpected guests or the all too rapid approach of an unprepared meal, lose their terror when you are supported by a tin of *Vol-au-Vents Cases* and a selection of tinned *Emergency Fillings* (p. 70) in your store cupboard. Then, all that is needed is the heating and assembling of the component parts.

If a quick vegetarian dish is wanted, you can make an *Egg Vol-au-Vent*.

Egg Vol-au-Vent 1   Oven Setting 375°F, Mark 5

For each serving allow:

1 *large Vol-au-Vent Case* (p. 41)	1½ *tablespoons Cheese Sauce* 1 *or* 2
1 *egg*	(pp. 7 and 85)
salt and pepper	or *Tomato Sauce* (pp. 85–6)

Break an egg into each case, and season to taste.
Bake in pre-heated oven until nearly set – about 15 to 20 minutes.
Cover egg with chosen sauce and return to the oven for a few minutes.

Egg Vol-au-Vent 2   Oven Setting 375°F, Mark 5

For each serving allow:

1 *large Vol-au-Vent Case* (p. 41)	*salt and pepper*
1 *tablespoon Cheese Foundation* (p. 7)	*finely grated cheese*
1 *egg*	

Spread the Cheese Foundation on the bottom of each case. Break egg on top of it, and season to taste. Cover with cheese and bake in pre-heated oven until the egg is set, about 20 minutes.

Egg Vol-au-Vent 3

This is the same as *Egg Vol-au-Vent* 2, except that *minced ham* is substituted for the Cheese Foundation.

SWEET TARTS AND FLANS

Plate Tarts

These can be made with short, rough puff or puff doughs. Roll puff thinly and only use it when making covered plate tarts. The cover will then be so good that the possibility of a slightly soggy base can be condoned.

For a thick, crisp surround to an open tart, roll the dough into a round with a diameter one to two inches larger than that of the plate. Lay this on the plate. Turn under the surplus dough. Press it down firmly and at the same time decorate, by using your thumb and cutting with a knife alternately. Most open tarts are greatly improved by a pastry lattice over the filling. Here is a quick, easy version. A small ball of extra dough is required – any odd scraps will do, when kneaded together. Flatten this ball into a circle. Using a little pastry cutting wheel, or a knife, starting in the centre, cut round and round towards the circumference, in ever widening circles, thus making a coil. Lift the centre of the coil on to the centre of the filling, then twisting and stretching the ribbon of dough, lay it on the tart in ever increasing circles.

For *covered plate tarts*, line the plate as given for open tarts, except the surplus dough is turned over and not under. The cover, also one to two inches larger in diameter, is placed over the filling and the surplus dough turned under. Press and decorate as explained for open tarts.

Sprinkle Short Crust covers with sugar about 10 minutes before the baking is completed.

Tart Fillings

The selection given on p. 45 is also suitable for plate tarts.

Apple tarts, pies and flans are always popular. Here are some with a difference. Other apple and pastry recipes are found on pp. 58–9.

Regency Apple Tart   Oven Setting 400°F, Mark 6

This exceptionally good tart was in vogue at the beginning of the nineteenth century. Then it was made with short crust, but it is equally delicious with rough puff, which is easier to manipulate.

For a 9 inch plate allow:

8 *oz Dough, Short* (pp. 33–4)	5 *fluid oz granulated sugar*
or *Rough puff* (pp. 34–5)	*mixed with* 1 *teaspoon cinnamon*
5 *cooking apples, peeled,*	
cored and cut into pieces	

Halve the dough, and roll out both pieces, keeping them as circular as possible, until they are slightly larger than the plate. Lift one piece on to the plate, and turn over the surplus dough. Place the apple on this and cover it with the remaining pastry. Again turn over the remaining dough.

Bake in pre-heated oven until the top begins to brown.

Remove tart from oven on to a working surface. Now comes the tricky part. Using a slice, carefully lift off the pastry lid, together with the pieces of apple adhering to it. Turn this over on to the working surface, apple side up. Don't worry if the pastry breaks and you can't get it off in one piece – it can always be patched up and no harm done. Shake about three quarters of the sugar and cinnamon over the apples on the plate. Mash this in with a fork.

Replace the pastry lid – apples still uppermost. Sprinkle with the remaining sugar mixture and return to the oven to brown.

Serve hot or cold with cream or custard. Ice cream is also an appreciated addition to a hot apple tart, and so is *Hard Lemon Sauce* (p. 82).

Swiss Apple Tart

Oven Setting 400°F, Mark 6

Short Crust Dough (pp. 33–4)
Apple Purée (pp. 132–3)
sugar to sweeten purée
(if necessary)
2–4 *oz currants*, according to size of tart

a few almonds, blanched and chopped
1 *or* 2 *eggs*, (according to size of tart)
2 *or* 4 *oz sugar*

Line a well-greased, loose-bottomed sandwich or shallow cake tin with the dough. Place in a basin sufficient apple purée almost to fill the lined tin. Sweeten apple to taste and add the currants and almonds. Use 1 egg for a small tart and 2 for a large one. Separate these – the whites into a basin and the yolks into the apple. Beat the mixture well, and pour it into the tin. Bake in pre-heated oven for about 15 minutes, or until set.

Remove from oven, cover with the meringue. (This must be made while the pie is baking, by whisking the egg white and folding in the sugar.)

Lower oven to 300°F, Mark 2, and bake tart for a further 15 to 20 minutes.

Serve cold. It is good and attractive when garnished with *whipped cream and cherries*.

Apple Crumb Flan

Oven Setting 375°F, Mark 5

4 *oz Short Crust Dough* (pp. 33–4)
½ pint *Apple Puree* (pp. 132–3)
2 *oz sugar*
½ *oz butter or margarine*

8 *fluid oz fresh breadcrumbs*
4 *fluid oz mixed dried fruit*
(*chopped*)
½ *teaspoon mixed spice*

Line a 7–8 inch flan tin, ring or foil dish with the dough.

Mix together all the other ingredients until well blended, then put the mixture into the pastry case.

Bake about 20 minutes in the pre-heated oven.
Serve hot or cold.

Apple Curd Flan   Oven Setting 375°F, Mark 5

a 7 to 8 inch Baked Pastry Case,   1 oz sugar
   Fleur or Short Crust (pp. 33,   ½ lb Apple Purée (pp. 132–3)
   37, 39, 40)   juice of 1 lemon (less if very juicy)
1 oz butter or margarine   1 egg, well beaten

Soften the butter and cream it with the sugar. Add the apple, lemon
juice and egg. Mix well and pour into the flan.
Bake 20 to 25 minutes in the pre-heated oven.
Serve hot or cold.

West Country Apple Treacle Tart   Oven Setting 375°F, Mark 5

8 oz Short Crust Dough (pp. 33–4)   Pinch each mixed spice and ground
½ pint brown breadcrumbs   ginger
1 lemon, juice and grated rind   ½ pint mixed currants and shredded
1 large apple, peeled, cored   peel (see p. 168)
   and coarsely grated   2 tablespoons golden syrup, warmed
                                            (if cold)

This is a covered tart. Divide the dough into two and roll out for an
8¾ inch pie plate or tin, as directed on p. 50. Grease tin and line it.
Blend all the other ingredients together, and fill crust with the mixture.
Cover with the remaining pastry.
Bake for about 30 minutes in pre-heated oven.
Serve hot or cold.

Currant Mint Tart   Oven Setting 400–475°F, Mark 6–9
                                             (according to dough used)

A very simple, but delicious, covered plate tart of North Country
origin.

   Short Crust, Rough Puff or   a few tablespoons demerara sugar
     Puff dough (pp. 33–37)   plenty of freshly chopped mint
   currants

Line, fill and cover plate as directed on p. 50.
Bake in pre-heated oven until brown.
Serve hot or cold.

Custard Pie   Oven Setting 325°F, Mark 3

To serve 2 allow:

a 6 inch Rough Puff, Short or Fleur   *5 fluid oz milk, warmed*
  Baked Pastry Case (pp. 33–5, 37, 39, 40) *1 large egg*
2 tablespoons sugar   *½ teaspoon vanilla or a little*
pinch of salt   *nutmeg*

Stir the sugar and salt into the milk. Beat in the egg until well blended. Add the flavouring and pour the mixture into a greased 6 inch metal or foil dish, similar to the one over which the case was baked.

Bake custard in pre-heated oven for 25 to 39 minutes, or until barely firm: cooking will continue as custard cools.

When the pie is to be served hot, heat the pastry case in the oven with the custard for the last 15 minutes of cooking. If to be eaten cold, the case may also need a spell in the oven to freshen it up.

Immediately before serving, loosen custard with a palette or ordinary knife, and slip it carefully into the case. Whether it is served hot or cold, only combine the two just before the pie is wanted – the pastry soon becomes soggy.

American Lemon Chiffon Pie

An extremely good party dish.

a large, freshly baked or re-heated   *4 egg yolks*
  Vol-au-Vent Flan or Puff Pastry   *6 oz sugar*
   Case (pp. 35–7, 39, 40, 42)   *3 teaspoons cornflour*
8 fluid oz boiling water   *4 tablespoons lemon juice*
1 tablespoon butter   *4 egg whites*
grated rind, 1 lemon   *Whipped Cream* (p. 105)

Put the boiling water, lemon rind and butter in the top of a double saucepan over boiling water, and heat.

Mix the egg yolks, sugar, cornflour and lemon juice in a basin.

In another basin, whisk the egg whites until very stiff.

Add the egg yolk mixture to the water, etc. in the pan, and stir until it thickens. Remove pan from heat, and fold in the egg whites. Chill or allow filling to cool before transferring it to the case. This should only be done shortly before serving: then top with whipped cream.

Lemon Curd Flans (see p. 71).

Fruit and Jelly Flans

These are especially good in *Fleur Pastry Cases*, but can also be made in any of the other baked cases (pp. 38–40).

Directions for making these fillings, with fresh or tinned fruit, are found on pp. 74–5.

Tartlets

A quick method of making tartlets, when the dough and the fillings are baked together, is as follows:

Use:

Short, Rough Puff or Puff Doughs

Roll the dough so that it is rectangular and a little larger than the sheet of patty pans to be used – these must not be too deep. Lay dough on this sheet and press it into each patty pan. Fill tartlets. Cut round the tin to even up the edges, and also cut both ways between all the patty pans, making squares. Fold the corners of each little square towards the centre of the filling.

The fillings given on p. 45 are also suitable for these tartlets.

SWEET TARTLETS

Congress Tarts   Oven Setting 400°F–450°F, Mark
                                      6–8 (according to dough used)

Short, Rough Puff or Puff   3 *oz ground almonds or ground*
  Pastry Doughs (pp. 33–37)   *rice*
raspberry jam   1 *egg*
2 *oz butter or margarine*   *a little almond essence*
2 *oz caster sugar*

Roll pastry thinly, line tart tins or foil cases, and spread the bottom of each with a little jam. Melt fat in a small saucepan. Add all the other ingredients. Mix them well, before putting a little of the filling on top of the jam.

Bake about 15–20 minutes in pre-heated oven.

Serve hot or cold.

Royal Tartlets   Oven Setting 450°F, Mark 8

about 6 oz Rough Puff or   *1 tablespoon caster sugar*
  Puff Dough (pp. 34–37)   *1 egg*
raspberry jam   *vanilla*
2 stale sponge cakes   *glacé cherries*
1½ oz butter or margarine,
  softened

Roll the pastry thinly, line the tart tins or foil cases, and put a little jam in the bottom of each. Rub the sponge cake through a sieve, or grate it.

Cream the butter and sugar in a basin. Separate the egg – the yolk into the fat and sugar, and the white into another basin. Stir the yolk and beat it well. Add the sponge cake crumbs and a little vanilla essence.

Whisk the egg white until stiff, then fold it into the mixture with a metal spoon. Put a little of this in each tartlet, enough to cover the jam.

Bake in pre-heated oven for about 15 to 20 minutes, until lightly browned. After 10 minutes, carefully place a piece of cherry on the centre of each.

When cold, sprinkle with *additional caster sugar*.

Chocolate Tartlets   Oven Setting 400°F–450°F, Mark
                                       6–8 (according to pastry used)

about 6 oz Short, Rough Puff *1 oz almonds, blanched and*
  or Puff Pastry Dough (pp. 33–   *chopped*
  37)   *1 oz flour*
apricot jam   *1 oz ground rice*
1½ oz softened butter or   *1 dessertspoon chocolate powder*
  margarine   *vanilla*
2 oz caster sugar
1 egg
Chocolate Icing (p. 165) *and a few almonds for decoration*

Roll pastry thinly, line the tart tins or foil cases, and put a little jam on the bottom of each. Cream the fat and sugar. Add the egg and beat well. Then add the almonds. Blend together the flour, ground rice and chocolate powder, and sieve them into the egg mixture. Add a few drops of vanilla and stir the filling lightly with a metal spoon. When well mixed, put a little in each tartlet, sufficient to three-quarter fill the crust.

Bake about 15 to 20 minutes in the pre-heated oven.

When cold, cover with a chocolate icing or couverture, and decorate with a few chopped almonds.

Plain or Spiced Cheese Cakes   Oven Setting 450°F, Mark 8

about 6 oz Rough Puff or   *a little lemon or vanilla essence,*
    Puff Pastry Dough (pp. 34–7)   *or* 1 *level teaspoon of cinnamon*
Lemon Filling (p. 71) *or*   3 *oz ground rice*
    lemon curd   *milk if required*
2 *oz caster sugar*   *sugar for dredging*
2 *oz butter or margarine*
1 *egg*

Roll pastry thinly, line the tart tins or foil cases and put a little lemon filling or curd on the bottom of each.

Cream the fat and sugar. Add the egg and beat well. For plain cheese cakes, stir in a drop or so of the essence, and for spiced, the cinnamon. Then add the ground rice and, if needed, a little milk. Stir the mixture again, very lightly with a metal spoon.

Put the filling into the tartlets, sufficient to three-quarter fill the crusts. Before putting the cheese cakes in the pre-heated oven, dredge them with sugar.

Bake for about 15–20 minutes.

Serve hot or cold.

Grape Tartlets   Oven Setting 375°F, Mark 5

These delicious, unusual tartlets hail from France. The following make 8 tartlets:

about 6 oz Short Crust Dough   2 *tablespoons golden syrup*
    (pp. 33–4)   1 *egg*
$\frac{1}{4}$ *lb grapes*

Roll the dough into 8 rounds of just over 3 inches. With these line the tart tins or foil cases, which must not be too shallow.

Peel grapes and remove pips; do this over a plate, not to lose any juice. (Should grapes refuse to cooperate, plunge them in boiling water for $\frac{1}{4}$–$\frac{1}{2}$ a minute; the skins will then come off easily.)

Measure the syrup into a small saucepan and warm it over a low heat until it is liquid. Add the egg and beat it into the syrup. Pour this mixture into the prepared tins, and drop in the grapes – 2 or 3 and a little juice in each.

Bake in the pre-heated oven 15 to 20 minutes, or until the tartlets are a pale brown.

Serve cold, when the mixture will be set.

More Pastry Dishes

Sausage Rolls Oven Setting 450–75°F, Mark 8–9

Sausage rolls are always popular, at home as well as at parties and picnics, and so little trouble to make. Of course you can make sausage rolls with skinless sausages and short or rough puff pastry, but we think they are far nicer made with:

sausage meat or
sausages with their skins removed and *Puff Pastry*

This is our procedure:
1. With well-floured hands roll the sausage meat, or the skinned sausages placed end to end, into long sausages.
2. Roll the dough into a rectangle. When using puff, it should be thin – $\frac{1}{8}$ inch at most.
3. Lay an elongated sausage on the front of the dough, equal in length to the width of the pastry. Leave about $\frac{1}{2}$ inch uncovered dough in front of the sausage.
4. Brush sausage with cold water.
5. Turn front edge of dough over the sausage.
6. Roll away from yourself until the sausage is covered with dough.
7. Cut the dough about $\frac{1}{2}$ inch away from the roll.
8. Brush edge with cold water, and complete the rolling operation.
9. Cut the long sausage roll into suitable lengths and lay them on a cold baking sheet.

Repeat stages 3 to 9 until all the sausage is used.
Bake about 15 minutes in pre-heated oven.
Serve hot or cold.

Fried Pies

How to make *Small Pies* is given on p. 44. Made with *Puff Pastry Dough* (pp. 35–37) these are delicious fried instead of baked. However, as

C.A.—C

they are rich, the fillings should be chosen with care. Use the less rich fillings given for Pasties, Turnovers and Small Pies (p. 45).

The pies are deep fried in *a good vegetable fat* at a temperature of 360–70°F until brown. Drain them on absorbent paper. Dredge savoury pies with *a little salt and paprika*, and sweet ones with *sugar*, mixed, if liked, with *a little spice*. Serve very hot.

The great advantage of fried pies is the speed in which they can be cooked and served, provided puff pastry dough and a suitable filling are to hand.

Each savoury pie needs about 3 oz of dough, which should be rolled into two 4½–5 inch rounds. Sweet pies are usually preferred smaller.

Beurrek

The recipe for this delicious Greek dish is on pp. 68–9.

Apple Dumplings

Oven setting according to the pastry dough used

With a supply of:

medium sized apples,
peeled and cored and *Short, Rough Puff or Puff Pastry Dough* (pp. 33–7)

apple dumplings are a good choice for the cook and consumer.

Cut a piece of dough for each apple, commensurate with its size. Roll this out thinly into rough squares, large enough to envelope the fruit. Place each apple on its square.

When it comes to filling the apples, you have a selection:

brown sugar, flavoured with cinnamon
or lemon peel and mixed with
softened butter,

mince meat,
Lemon Filling (p. 71),
or any other of the Sweet
Fillings (given on p. 45)

Having filled the apples and spread a little of the filling on the outsides, moisten the pastry edges and press them together on top of the apples.

Place the dumplings in an oven of the correct heat for the dough used. As soon as the pastry begins to brown, lower heat to 325°F, Mark 3, and continue to bake until the fruit is soft – about 30 minutes in all. Dredge with sugar for the last few minutes of baking.

Serve hot or cold. Apple dumplings are good with *Cream* (p. 105), *Ice Cream* (p. 190) or a suitable *Hard Sauce* (p. 82).

Crusty Apple Roll
Oven Setting 400°F, Mark 6

THE ROLL:

½ lb Short Crust Dough
(pp. 33–4)
about 1 lb apples, peeled,
cored and thinly sliced

2 tablespoons sugar
½ teaspoon cinnamon or
ground ginger

Roll out the pastry into an oblong on a piece of floured greaseproof paper. Cover with apple and sprinkle with the sugar mixed with the chosen spice.
Roll up like a Swiss Roll and put in a greased oven dish.

THE SAUCE:

4 tablespoons warmed golden syrup
4 tablespoons sugar
6 tablespoons boiling water

a knob of butter
2 cloves

Blend the ingredients thoroughly, then pour the sauce over the roll.
Bake in pre-heated oven for ½ hour, or until brown, and baste with the sauce two or three times during the baking.
Serve hot or cold.

Mock Apple Strudel
Oven Setting 450°F, Mark 8

To serve 4, allow:

½–¾ lb Rough Puff Pastry Dough
(pp. 34–5)
12 oz cooking apples, peeled,
cored and finely chopped
2 oz sultanas
2 oz moist brown sugar

1 teaspoon cinnamon
1½ oz hazel nuts or blanched
almonds, finely chopped
milk
icing sugar

Roll out the pastry on a piece of floured greaseproof paper, into an oblong of about 12 by 7 inches and ⅛ inch thick. Cover this with the apple, sultanas, brown sugar, cinnamon and 1 oz of the nuts. Roll it up like a Swiss roll. Pinch the two ends together and seal the flap with cold water.
Place on a baking sheet. Bake in pre-heated oven for 10 minutes.

Remove strudel, brush with milk and sprinkle with the rest of the nuts. Reduce heat to 350°F, Mark 4, and continue the cooking until the apples are soft and the top browned.

Cut a small slice from each end, and sprinkle with icing sugar.

Serve hot with *Whipped Cream* (p. 105), or cold as a cake.

New Zealand Milk Pudding   Oven Setting 375°F, Mark 5

This pudding is a 'go as you please' one with regard to quantities, yet always turns out to everyone's satisfaction.

Short Crust or Rough Puff Dough	*fresh breadcrumbs*
(pp. 33–35)	*dried fruit* (optional)
golden syrup	*milk*

Roll the dough into an oblong. Cover this with syrup, then a layer of crumbs. Sprinkle on the fruit if you want it – just as much as you fancy.

Roll it up into a Swiss roll and put into a not too shallow, greased, oblong or oval pie dish. Just cover with milk.

Bake for about 30 minutes in the pre-heated oven or until nice and brown.

Serve hot.

Puff Pastry Slices

How these are made is explained on p. 42. Hot or cold they make a grand sweet. Slice them into three, so you can have two layers of filling. *Jam, lemon curd* or the fillings given for *Pastry Cases* (pp. 71–73) can all be used, and when a slice of *Ice Cream* (p. 190) is also incorporated, you certainly have a sweet to be proud of.

Slices should all be topped with *whipped cream* (p. 105).

FILLINGS AND SPREADS

Savoury Fillings and Spreads

MOST of the following Fillings and Spreads will keep well in a refrigerator for several days – some considerably longer.
The same fillings can often be used in varied dishes:
for example, in vol-au-vents or in stuffed pancakes
in turn-overs or in fritters or spread on toast, etc.
When preparing one of these adaptable fillings, it is well to bear in mind your plans for the near future and to budget accordingly for the quantities needed.

Shell Fish Filling   For: Baked pastry cases
                                                Pancakes

Serve hot or cold.
Can be prepared in advance.
This useful filling can be made from a choice of:
prawns – scampi – shrimps – crab – lobster
(fresh, frozen or tinned)
The chosen shell fish is mixed with either
one of the Savoury Cream Sauces on pp. 85–87
(a little Sour Cream, p. 105, is good mixed with the sauce)
or
Canadian Mayonnaise, p. 99
Heat filling in a double saucepan and add
a little chopped parsley or chervil

Tuna Fish and Cheese Filling   For: Baked pastry cases
                                                Pancakes

Serve hot.
Can be prepared in advance.
> *a tin of tuna fish*
> *Cheese Sauce 1 (p. 7)*
> or
> *Cheese Sauce 2 (p. 85).*
> *half as much sauce as fish*

61

Drain the fish. Mash it well with a fork and work in the sauce.
Heat in a double saucepan.

Fish Cream Filling   For: Baked pastry cases
                                          Pancakes

Serve hot or cold.
Can be prepared in advance.

To serve 2–3 allow:

> ½ *lb fresh fillet or a small packet of frozen fillet*
> 3–4 *tablespoons Basic Cream Sauce* (p. 84)
> *salt and pepper to taste*
> *about* 1 *teaspoon of anchovy essence*
> *a little Single Cream, Sour Cream* (p. 105) *or top milk*
> 2 *tablespoons chopped parsley or dill*
> *either* 1 *chopped hard boiled egg*
> *or* 2–3 *tablespoons shelled shrimps, fresh, frozen or tinned*

If the fish is frozen, thaw out well before cooking.

Measure the sauce into the top of a double saucepan, and place over
gentle heat, stirring with a wooden spoon until soft and smooth. Add
the seasoning and stir in the anchovy.

Lay the fish, skin uppermost, on top of the sauce; sprinkle on a little
salt and pepper. Cover pan and place it over the lower pan containing
boiling water. Steam for 15 minutes or until the fish is cooked. Then
carefully lift it on to a plate and remove skin and any bones.

Blend fish juices into the sauce and add sufficient cream or milk to
make it the right consistency. Stir in the herb and either the egg or
shrimps. Flake fish and fold it carefully into the sauce.

If filling is to be used immediately, reheat sauce to boiling point before
incorporating the fish.

After storing, reheat filling in a double saucepan.

Salmon Spread   For: Canapés and Spreads
Can be prepared in advance.

> *a* 7–8 *oz tin of salmon*   ¼ *teaspoon lemon juice, fresh*
> 2 *tablespoons Mayonnaise*   *or bottled*
>   (p. 98)   *salt and pepper to taste*
> 1 *oz softened butter*   1 *dessertspoon chopped parsley*

Drain the liquid from the fish and remove any bones,

Mash the salmon with a fork and add the other ingredients. Work them in until blended and the mixture is creamy.

Sardine Filling and Spread

Serve hot or cold.
Can be prepared in advance.

For: Baked pastry cases, pasties, small pies, two crust tarts, canapés, sandwiches.

a tin of sardines, about 200 grms
1½ heaped tablespoons flour
salt and pepper to taste

a tin of sweet red peppers, about 5 oz
2½ fluid oz warm water
1 tablespoon chopped parsley

Strain off all the sardine oil into a small saucepan, and put the sardines on a plate. Mix the flour and seasoning into the oil with a wooden spoon and cook over medium heat. Allow to boil for about a minute. Remove pan from heat.

Strain all the liquor from the red peppers into the pan and put the peppers on the plate with the sardines. Stir the pepper juice and the water into the oil mixture and cook it until it boils and thickens. Mash the sardines and peppers together with a fork until smooth and well blended. Then mix in the sauce from the pan and the parsley.

Salmon or Tuna Fish Filling and Spread

Serve hot or cold.
Can be prepared in advance.

For: Baked pastry cases, pasties, small pies (baked and fried), two crust tarts, fritters, canapés, sandwiches.

a 6–7 oz tin of fish
1 oz butter or margarine
1 small onion, grated
2 tablespoons flour
salt and pepper to taste

milk
1 tablespoon vinegar (preferably garlic
or tarragon vinegar)
1 tablespoon chopped parsley
1 hard boiled egg, chopped

Drain the fish over a measure to catch the liquid. Melt the fat in a small pan and cook the onion until clear. Remove pan from heat, and stir in the flour and seasoning with a wooden spoon, mix well, and cook for two minutes.

Add milk to the fish liquor in the measure so that together they amount to 5 fluid oz. Gradually stir this liquid into the mixture in the pan. Replace over heat, and stir until it thickens. Remove from heat and blend in the vinegar, parsley and egg. Lastly fork in the fish, making sure there are no bones.

Chill before using.

Cornish Pasty Filling

Serve hot or cold.
Can be prepared in advance.

For: Pasties, small pies (baked or fried), two crust tarts, fritters.

This is a good way of finishing the remains of roast joints, though it can also be made with tinned meats. It is a dish that must be 'played off the cuff' where quantities are concerned. How many vegetables are used is decided by the gap between the meat at your disposal and the size and number of pasties or fritters that you hope to make.

Here is a filling made from 4 oz meat which should give 3 to 4 portions.

½ oz butter, margarine or dripping
1 small onion, shredded
3 teaspoons flour
2½ fluid oz left-over gravy or
    stock
salt, pepper and Worcester sauce
    to taste

2 medium sized potatoes, pressure-
    cooked or steamed (p. 144)
4 oz cooked meat
4 cooked Brussel sprouts or
    a few cooked French beans

Melt the fat in a saucepan and cook the onion until clear. Add the flour, stir it in with a wooden spoon and cook for two minutes, stirring all the time. Remove pan from heat, and gradually mix in the liquid. Cook again, still stirring until the sauce thickens. Add the seasonings.

Skin the potatoes and cut them into little cubes.

If the meat is really tender, cut that also into little cubes, otherwise put it through a hand or electric shredder.

Slice the sprouts or cut up the beans.

Mix the meat and vegetable into the sauce and chill well before using.

Curry Filling

Serve hot or cold.
Can be prepared in advance.

For: Baked pastry cases, pasties, curry puffs (made with puff pastry), small pies (baked or fried), two crust tarts, fritters.

This, like Cornish Pasty Filling, is an excellent way of finishing that odd bit of meat, and fish too. It can also be made with tins of meat or fish, but in this quite delicious filling, the meat or fish have little importance; the flavour relies on the character and assortment of the other ingredients. Again, like Cornish Pasty Filling, Curry Filling must be 'played off the cuff', and the kinds and quantities of foods used must be regulated by requirements, inclination, and ingredients to hand.

Here is the base of a curry filling to serve about 4–5:

1 *oz butter or margarine*	1–2 *dessertspoons curry powder*
1 *large onion, finely sliced*	½ *teaspoon salt*
1 *large cooking apple, peeled,*	1 *dessertspoon black treacle or*
cored and sliced	*marmalade*
1 *clove garlic, crushed*	1 *dessertspoon chutney*
1 *tablespoon flour*	6 *fluid oz milk*

Melt the fat in a saucepan and cook the onion for about two minutes. Add the apple and garlic. Cover pan and cook over a gentle heat until the apple is mushy. Remove from heat, and stir in the flour, curry powder and salt. Cook for a minute, stirring with a wooden spoon. Add the remaining ingredients, and cook the mixture again until it thickens. To this base are added any of the following:

cooked meat, cut in little cubes,	*dried fruit*
shredded or minced	*banana, sliced*
cooked fish, flaked	*oranges, cut in small pieces*
salted nuts	*grapes, peeled and pipped*
hard boiled egg, chopped	*pineapple cut in small pieces*
mixed pickles, chopped	*green and red peppers (fresh or*
	tinned), cut in thin slices

Chill well before baking or frying.

Casseroled Game, Poultry or Meat   For: baked pastry cases
Fillings   Pancakes

Serve hot.

Can be prepared in advance.

Game, poultry and meat in good, thick, creamy sauce, make excellent fillings for vol-au-vents, pastry flans and pancakes. Most well cooked casserole dishes answer this description, and can either be prepared especially as a filling, or, as left overs, will be appreciated in their new pastry or pancake setting.

Whether newly cooked or reheated, strain the casserole over a saucepan and tip the solids on to a plate. If they are cumbersome, cut the meat and vegetables into neat pieces.

Bring the sauce to boiling point. Should there be more sauce than is needed for the filling, i.e. about half as much sauce as solids, pour the surplus into a sauce boat. Mix the meat and vegetables with the balance and bring the lot just up to simmering point. Keep the filling and extra sauce hot until just before serving.

Hot Kidney Filling   For: Baked pastry cases
                                     Pancakes

Do not store. Serve immediately.

This is really a light luncheon or supper dish in its own right, and can always be served on toast or in a surround of *Creamed Potato* (p. 115). Still it makes such a special dish when served in vol-au-vents, flans, other pastry cases or in pancakes that it had to be included here.

To serve 2 allow:

4 *lambs' kidneys*	*or* ½–1 *red or green pepper, seeded*
½ *teaspoon flour*	*and sliced*
salt and pepper to taste	*or* 2 *large or* 4 *small tomatoes,*
2 *oz butter*	*peeled and sliced*
either ¼ *lb mushrooms*	1 *teaspoon chopped parsley*
cleaned (p. 91)	*a few drops of lemon juice, fresh or bottled*
and sliced	½ *glass sherry* (*optional*)

Cut the kidneys into halves, and each half into three. Sprinkle these with the flour and seasoning.

Melt the butter in a fairly small pan. When hot, add the kidneys and the prepared chosen vegetable. Stir continuously with a wooden spoon, and cook fairly quickly for 3 to 4 minutes – no longer, or the kidneys will toughen. Lastly add the parsley, lemon juice and sherry. Give the final stir, at the same time scraping the bottom of the pan.

Fill the hot cases or pancakes and serve.

Hot Liver and Bacon Filling   For: Baked pastry cases
                                              Pancakes

Do not store. Serve immediately.

This is akin to the kidney filling, can well be served on its own, but is quite delicious in vol-au-vents, flans, other pastry cases or pancakes.

To serve 2 allow:

1 *oz butter*	*either* ¼ *lb mushrooms, cleaned*
1 *teaspoon olive oil*	(p. 91) *and chopped finely*
2 *rashers streaky bacon,*	*or* 1 *red or green pepper, seeded*
cut into strips	*and chopped finely*
1 *small onion, grated*	*or* 2 *large or* 4 *small tomatoes,*
4 *oz lamb's or calf's liver,*	*skinned and chopped finely*
cut into thin 1 *inch strips*	1 *tablespoon chopped parsley*
1 *tablespoon flour*	*a pinch of mixed dried herbs*
¼ *teaspoon salt*	*a little lemon juice, fresh or*
pepper to taste	*bottled*

Melt the butter and oil in a saucepan over gentle heat and cook the bacon and onion, until they are both clarified.

In the meantime, shake the liver in a paper bag with the flour and seasoning. When the bacon is cooked, add the liver. Stir it with a wooden spoon and as soon as it changes colour, add all the other ingredients. Lower the heat a little and cook for a further 3 minutes, still stirring to prevent sticking.

Fill hot cases or pancakes and serve.

Mushroom Filling   For: Baked pastry cases
                              Pancakes
Serve hot.
Can be prepared in advance.

To serve 2–3 allow:

1 *oz butter*	*grated nutmeg (optional)*
1 *tablespoon olive oil*	1 *tablespoon grated onion*
½ *lb mushrooms, cleaned*	1 *tablespoon chopped parsley*
(p. 91) *and sliced*	3 *or 4 tablespoons cream or*
salt and pepper	*top milk*

Heat butter and oil in a frying pan over gentle heat, and cook the mushrooms for a minute, stirring with a wooden spoon.

Add the seasoning, onion, parsley and cream or top milk. Still stirring gently with a wooden spoon, continue the cooking, but not longer than 4 minutes.

Either fill cases or pancakes and serve or store.

Mushroom and Egg Filling   For: Baked pastry cases
                                       Pancakes
Serve hot.
Can be prepared in advance.

To serve 2–3:

As for the above *Mushroom Filling*, with the addition of:

1 *or 2 chopped hard boiled eggs*

This is added to the mushrooms with the seasoning, onion and parsley.

Bacon and Egg Filling and Spread   For: Baked pastry cases, pasties, small pies (baked or fried), two crust tarts, fritters, canapés spreads

Serve hot or cold.
Can be prepared in advance.

To serve 4–5 allow:

4 rashers streaky bacon, cut up
4 eggs
plain flour
1 teaspoon dry mustard
pepper to taste
milk

tomato ketchup or Worcester sauce
    or Canadian Mayonnaise (p. 99)
chopped parsley
chopped chives (optional)
finely grated parmesan (optional)

Cook the bacon on the top of a double saucepan over boiling water, until a lot of fat has exuded. While the bacon is cooking, hard boil the eggs. Remove bacon pan from heat and discard the lower saucepan.

Stir a little flour into the bacon fat – enough to absorb it. Add the mustard and pepper. Return to the heat and cook for a minute.

Now slowly add and stir in the liquid, sufficient to make the sauce the consistency of a thin custard. The liquid should be made up of milk and a little ketchup, sauce or mayonnaise.

Return the pan to the heat, and cook slowly, stirring all the time until the mixture thickens. Still stirring, allow the sauce to simmer for a few minutes before removing it from the heat. Chop or slice the eggs and add them and all the remaining ingredients to the sauce.

Test the flavour and chill before baking or frying.

Leberwurst and Cheese Filling and Spread

For: Canapés, spreads

Serve cold.
Can be made in advance.

Blend together equal quantities of:
Leberwurst and either *Cheese Foundation* (p. 7) *with chopped parsley*
                or *Cream Cheese with chopped parsley or chives* (pp. 110–111).

Croquette Mixture (pp. 92–4) Filling

Any of these mixtures can be cooked in pasties, small pies, or fritters.

Beurrek Filling

For: Pasties, small pies (baked or fried), fritters, croquettes

Serve hot.
Can be made in advance.

This pleasant but simple filling is taken from a Greek recipe. In that country the mixture is rolled into little sausages, wrapped in very thin pastry and fried in hot oil. It is, however, just as good in any shape and baked; provided the pastry is very thin, any dough can be used. Beurrek Filling also makes excellent fritters or croquettes.

To serve 2–3 allow:

¼ lb Gruyère, Emmenthal   3 tablespoons Basic Cream Sauce
or Jarlsberg   (p. 84)

Cut the cheese into small pieces and heat it with the sauce in a small saucepan, non-stick if possible, over gentle heat. Stir continuously until blended.

Pour mixture into a dish and chill before using. Serve hot.

Ham and Cheese Filling and Spread

For: Baked pastry cases, pasties, small pies (baked or fried), fritters, canapés, sandwiches

Serve hot or cold.
Can be prepared in advance.
This is a good way of using up the remains of ham and bacon joints.

Mince the *ham or bacon* and mix in enough *Cheese Foundation* (p. 7) or *Cream Cheese* (p. 110) to be able to handle or spread the mixture.

Egg and Cheese Filling and Spread

For: Baked pastry cases, pasties, small pies (baked or fried), fritters, canapés, sandwiches

Serve hot or cold.
Can be prepared in advance.

Hard boiled eggs, chopped
about the same quantity Cheese Foundation (p. 7)
or Cream Cheese (pp. 110–11)
a little of any of the following:
chopped parsley, chervil, chives, pickles, olives, anchovy
Blend together all the ingredients.

Cheese Spreads

For: Canapés, sandwiches

Can be prepared in advance.

Cheese Foundation (p. 7) *with a little chopped parsley*
or Cream Cheese savoury (p. 110)

Minute vol-au-vent cases and small savoury fleur pastry cases filled with this mixture make excellent canapés. Likewise small cheese biscuits and croûtons. All these should be decorated with colourful tit-bits such as:

> *shrimps, prawns, slivers of anchovy, halved stuffed olives, small slices of pineapple, chopped salted peanuts, halved cocktail onions, slices of cocktail gherkins.*

Anchovy or Tomato Cheese Spread

For: Canapés, sandwiches

This is the same as for the above recipe, except anchovy essence or tomato purée is added to the Cheese Foundation or Cream Cheese – enough to give a pleasing colour and nice flavour.

Portuguese Spread

For: Canapés, sandwiches

This interesting spread is made with:

anchovies, chopped	*chopped flesh of a skinned tomato,*
gherkins, chopped	*no pips*
parsley, chopped	*hard boiled egg, chopped*
chives or spring onions, chopped,	*Cheese Foundation* (p. 7)
or onion, grated	*or Cream Cheese* (pp. 110–11)
a few capers, chopped	*a pinch of chilli pepper*

Mix the anchovy with the vegetables and the egg. Bind these together with the cheese and add the chilli pepper.

Herb Butters – p. 77

For sandwiches

Softened *Herb Butter* can add a welcome flavour when used in sandwiches.

Emergency Filling

For baked pastry cases

You can face any emergency with tins of:
fish – meat – creamed mushrooms – sweetcorn, cream style – sweet red peppers – tomatoes – any of the condensed soups together with: *a tin of your own pastry cases.*

A tin of fish or meat blended with one of the creamed vegetables or with peppers or tomatoes and one of the condensed soups, makes a good filling and this, served in vol-au-vent cases, provides a substantial main dish, which can be served hot or cold.

Sweet Fillings

When you have pastry cases in your store cupboard, pastry doughs in your refrigerator and Cake Foundation in your larder, a few available sweet fillings will ensure, at very short notice, a good selection of flans, tarts, tartlets, small pies (baked or fried), turnovers and puddings. These fillings can also be used for pancakes.

Lemon Filling and Instant Lemon Curd

This is a most useful, versatile filling and, when made with Cake Foundation, is particularly quick to prepare. If fresh eggs are used, it will keep at least 3 weeks in a cool place, longer in a refrigerator, and more or less indefinitely in a deep freeze. Those with a deep freeze may prefer to make a large quantity of this filling to store in cartons.

For a household of 2 allow:

4 *oz butter or margarine, warmed*   2 *eggs*
4 *oz caster sugar*   *juice of* 1 *or* 2 *lemons*
rind of 1 *lemon, grated and*
   crushed with 1 *tablespoon sugar*

Cream the fat, sugar and lemon sugar until very light and fluffy. Beat the eggs together in a basin. Add these and the lemon juice alternately to the creamed butter and sugar, a little at a time.

The same recipe made with Cake Foundation:

10 *oz Cake Foundation*   1 *egg*
rind of 1 *lemon, grated and*   *juice of* 1 *or* 2 *lemons*
   crushed with 1 *tablespoon sugar*

Lemon Filling, as much or as little as is needed, can be easily changed into *Lemon Curd*, by putting the required quantity into the top of a double saucepan and cooking it over boiling water.

When Lemon Filling is cooked in baked pastry cases, it will need about 20 minutes, or until the filling has become a curd and is just beginning to brown, in an oven of 325°F, Mark 3. *Fleur Lemon Curd Flans* or *Tartlets* must be served cold – the others can be eaten hot or cold.

When *Lemon Filling* is baked or steamed with uncooked pastry dough or sponge batter, it will comply with the temperature and timing of the recipe in which it is used.

Date, Walnut and Lemon Filling

> *Chopped dates*   *chopped walnuts*   *Lemon Filling*

Cherry Lemon Filling

> *chopped glace cherries*   *Lemon Filling*

Apple Purée

Apple Purée (pp. 132–3) is an excellent flan and tartlet filling, and features in a number of pastry, sponge and pancake recipes. The 'Cook Ahead with Apples' section tells how you can always have a jar of purée in your store cupboard. However, seeing that variety is a cook's trump card, you may like to serve *Apple Purée* in different ways.

Apple Compôte

For recipe, see p. 134.

Apple and Sherry Filling

This filling is especially good served in cases made with Almond Cinnamon Pastry (p. 38), and when these are topped with whipped cream, you have a good party dish.

To fill about 4 tartlet cases allow:

> 1 *sponge cake*   4 *tablespoons Apple Purée*
> 2 *tablespoons sherry*   *sugar to taste*
> 1 *tablespoon ground almonds,*
>   *more if wished*

Crumble the sponge cakes and soak the crumbs in the sherry. When the alcohol is all absorbed, mix in the remaining ingredients.

Apple, Jam and Cake-crumb Filling

To *each tablespoon of Apple Purée*, allow:

> 1 *tablespoon jam*   2 *tablespoons stale cake-crumbs*

Apple, Raspberry and Coconut Filling

To each 3 *tablespoons of Apple Purée* allow:

> 2 *tablespoons raspberry jam*   2 *tablespoons desiccated coconut*

Apple, Ginger and Nut Filling

Mix according to taste:
Apple Purée   chopped preserved ginger   chopped walnuts

Butterscotch Sauce

The recipe is on p. 80. As well as a sauce, this is an excellent filling.

Butterscotch Nut Flan and Tartlet Filling

This can be served in any type of pastry case, but when used to fill fleur cases makes a party dish.
Fill cases with *Butterscotch Sauce* and top with:
Fried Almonds
These are prepared as follows:
Blanch *almonds* and dry on absorbent paper. Chop them coarsely. Fry in *hot butter* until a golden brown.
Sprinkle almonds with *sugar* and fry them for a further few minutes. Turn on to absorbent paper to cool.

Butterscotch Crunch

To each tablespoon *Butterscotch Sauce* allow:
2 *digestive biscuits*
Crumble the biscuits and mix with the sauce.
This filling is nice as it is, but perhaps more interesting with the addition of one or more of the following:
chopped nuts   chopped dates
chopped preserved ginger,   shredded candied peel, see
including a little syrup   p. 168

Rum Butter Filling

This is a special party filling for *Fleur and Almond Cinnamon Flan and Tartlet Cases.*

Add to the *Rum Butter* (p. 82) as many of the following as you choose:
Chopped walnuts or any   chopped dates
other nuts   chopped crystallized pineapple
chopped glacé cherries   or other crystallized fruit
shredded candied peel

Cream Cheese and Kirsch (p. 111)

Jelly Fillings for Flans and Tartlets

These can be savoury or fruit fillings to fit cases of any size, made of any of the pastry doughs. The only proviso being that the fillings must be set in tins or dishes similar to those used for baking the flan or tartlet cases in which they are to be served – see pp. 39–40. Alcan foil dishes or baking cases are as good for setting the jellies as they are for baking the cases – the jelly can be ejected so easily.

Vol-au-vent cases are not suitable for jelly fillings, but vol-au-vent flan cases (p. 42) are excellent. When these are to be used, make the jelly filling in a tin of the same size as the smaller plate used, or when a tin was used for cutting out the flan centre, you have no problem, use that.

The appeal of these fillings depends as much on appearance as taste. *The Foods* must be colourful, of pleasing shapes and arranged attractively.

The Jelly must just cover the food and harmonize in colour and flavour.

For each ¼ pint cold liquid allow 1 *teaspoon powdered gelatine*

Put the gelatine in a cup or small basin. Pour over a little of the cold liquid – just enough to cover the gelatine – and leave to soak for a few minutes. Boil up the remaining liquid and dissolve in it the soaked gelatine. Stir well and pour jelly over the arranged food.

Chill and store until just before the flans or tartlets are to be served. Then, with the help of a palette or pliable knife, slip the jelly filling out of the tin or dish into the awaiting pastry cases.

Savoury Jelly Fillings

An excellent summer first course is provided by individual savoury jelly flans served on a good salad. The 4½ inch Alcan foil dishes are just right for these.

The following foods are good in savoury fillings:
tinned prawns or *shrimps – strips of cold ham – slices of cooked breast of chicken – tinned asparagus tips – stuffed olives – tinned sweet red peppers – cooked green peas – slices of hard boiled egg.*

For the savoury jelly, any of the following can be used, with or without water as necessary:
the liquor from any tinned foods – ham stock – chicken stock – a little lemon juice or vinegar

To improve the jelly's colour a little tomato purée can be added to the boiling liquor.

Fruit Jelly Fillings

Fresh or tinned fruit can be used.
For the Fruit Jelly
With fresh fruit use:
   water and a little jam to give flavour and colour
or
    ¼ *sherry or sweet wine and* ¾ *water*
Jam can also be added to the alcohol mixture. It must be added to the boiling liquid, which should be strained before it is used to dissolve the soaked gelatine.
 With tinned fruit, the liquid is made up by:
    the fruit's syrup and water
or
   syrup and sherry or sweet wine, and water
If wished, a little red or orange colouring essence can be introduced.

Tinned Fruit Pie Fillings (store cupboard fillings)

Many of these commercial fruit fillings are very good, and it certainly pays to stock a few tins of your favourites to serve in your home made flans and tartlet cases, in emergencies. One of our favourite instant sweets – fit for any occasion – is a cherry filling in a fleur flan topped with *whipped cream*.

Apple and Lemon or Orange Flan and Tartlet Filling

This is not a filling that keeps, but can be made in a moment provided you have the apples and some Lemon or Orange Syrup (p. 83). It is good in any baked pastry case and especially so in fleur flan or tartlet cases.
 The filling is also nice eaten with a cereal or mixed with *Sweet Fried Crumbs* (p. 201) and served with cream.

 It is made with:
   dessert apples and Lemon or Orange Syrup
Mix the syrup with freshly grated apples. They will not discolour.

SAUCE SECTION

THIS is an important section, as not only can interesting sauces and dressings add interest to dull dishes, and make good dishes even better, but sauces often feature extensively in recipes.

SAVOURY AND SWEET SAUCES

Any spare moment spent in making one of these sauces is sure to be appreciated in the days to come. They play a useful part in the Cook Ahead programme.

SAVOURY LONG-KEEPING SAUCES

Mustard Sauce 1*

This sauce, so quick and simple to prepare, keeps for weeks, can be served hot or cold, and is delicious with fish, pork, bacon, ham, sausages and salads.

2 *hard-boiled eggs*	2 *tablespoons vinegar (garlic*
2 *tablespoons olive oil*	*vinegar if available)*
4 *teaspoons German or French mustard*	1 *tablespoon chopped parsley*
1 *tablespoon sugar*	1 *tablespoon grated onion*
¼ *teaspoon salt*	1 *dessertspoon chopped chives*
a little freshly milled pepper	*or other green herbs*

Place the egg yolks in a small basin and crush them with a wooden spoon. Gradually stir in the oil, to make a smooth paste. Add the mustard, sugar and seasoning, and, still stirring, gradually incorporate the vinegar. An electric liquidizer will blend the egg yolks, oil, mustard, sugar, seasoning and vinegar in one operation.

Chop the egg whites very finely. Add these, the parsley, onions and herbs, or, when using a liquidizer, incorporate the egg white and other ingredients mechanically.

Store the sauce in a covered container, in a refrigerator or cool place.

* *Mustard Sauce 2*, p. 86, is made with Basic Cream Sauce.

Horseradish Sauce 1*

This is made with *Mustard Sauce* 1 and Heinz' Dried Horseradish. Dried Horseradish is one of the 57 varieties, but sometimes difficult to obtain: however, retailers should be able to produce it when pressed. As well as serving Horseradish Sauce with beef, try cooking it in *Sliced Meat Fritters* (p. 19).

> 1 *teaspoon dried horseradish*   4 *teaspoons Mustard Sauce 1*
> 1½ *teaspoons milk*

Mix the horseradish and milk. Cover and let stand for at least 10 minutes before adding the Mustard Sauce.

This sauce can also be made by using *Mayonnaise* 1 *or* 2, *Mayonnaise Sauce or Canadian Mayonnaise* (pp. 98–9) instead of *Mustard Sauce*. However when using *Mayonnaise* 1 or 2 the Horseradish Sauce must not be cooked.

Herb Butter

To each ¼ lb of softened butter add:

1 *tablespoon chopped parsley*	1 *clove garlic, crushed*
1 *tablespoon chopped chives or*	*(optional)*
grated onion	¼ *teaspoon paprika*
½ *teaspoon each chopped fresh or*	*salt and pepper to taste*
a pinch dried savory, marjoram	*a little lemon juice, fresh*
basil, tarragon	*or bottled (optional)*

Blend well and pack in covered jars or cartons. It will keep for weeks in a refrigerator and more or less indefinitely in a deep freeze. Serve in little individual cubes or small balls, fashioned with butter pats, on fish, steak, chops, potatoes or other vegetables. Herb Butter can also be used for sandwiches (see p. 70).

The given recipe is a delicious blend, but can be varied according to taste. A nice *'Green Butter'* is made with:

> *about 4 tablespoons chopped parsley – seasoning –*
> *and a little lemon juice*

Sauce Indienne   A liquidizer sauce

To ¼ lb softened butter allow:

2 *hard boiled eggs, chopped*	½ *teaspoon curry powder*
1 *teaspoon dark, moist sugar*	*salt to taste* (with unsalted butter)

* *Horseradish Sauce 2*, p. 89, is made with Basic Cream Sauce.

Blend the ingredients in a liquidizer. Store sauce in covered container in refrigerator or cool place. It should keep at least a month. Serve hot with fish, meat or vegetables and potatoes. See *Potatoes à l'Indienne* (p. 123). Also delicious mixed with fried or grilled chipolatas and boiled long grain rice – see p. 123: this makes a good supper dish.

Mayonnaise and Salad Dressings

These are all found on pp. 98–102.

Manie Butter (Beurre Manie)

This is not a sauce, but is likely to be a godsend when you make your sauces. With Manie Butter in your refrigerator, you have a quick, ready to use thickening agent and need never worry should a sauce or gravy be too thin. Just add a little of this butter mixture to your hot liquid and let it come to the boil, but not actually boil.

Cream together butter and flour in the proportion of:
> 1 *tablespoon butter* to 1 *teaspoon flour*

Make enough for the next week or two.

Mint Jelly

This again is not a sauce, but it is a perennial equivalent to mint sauce and also keeps for years. Three generations of our family would regard a joint of lamb as sadly lacking without Mint Jelly.

Where quantities are concerned, it is one of those nice, go as you please, recipes, and is made with:

apples (*windfalls will do*)	mint (*as much as you can manage*)
vinegar and water, *in equal parts*	sugar

Wash the apples – no need to peel or core them. Cut them up roughly, put them in a preserving pan or large saucepan and cover them with the vinegar and water mixture. The mint that you have picked, been given or bought, will unfortunately not be at its best when the apples are available, so you will have to make the most of it. Wash and dry it carefully. Pick off all the respectable leaves, put them in a polythene bag and store in a cool place till the next day. Roughly cut up the stalks and add them and the remaining leaves to the apples. Cook until the apples are completely mushy. Drain off juice, and let the apple mixture drip all night, either through a cloth or a large hair sieve.

Next day, measure the juice and put it in the preserving pan or saucepan. Heat 1 lb of sugar for every pint of juice. Finely chop the mint leaves. Heat the juice and add the warm sugar and stir until the sugar has dissolved. Boil rapidly. Shortly before it is likely to set, add the mint.

When the mixture has jelled, pour it into hot jars. Cover when cold.

SWEET LONG-KEEPING SAUCES

Chocolate Sauce 1

This very popular sauce is quick to prepare. It can be reheated, but, unlike *Chocolate Sauce 2*, must not be baked or boiled. It is delicious with *Ice Cream Sundaes* (pp. 193-5) and can make everyday sweets into something special. Try it with a cornflour mould or a creamy milk pudding.

> 1 *oz butter or margarine*   2½ *tablespoons sugar*
> 2 *level tablespoons cocoa*   ¼ *teaspoon vanilla*
> 2 *tablespoons water*

Put all the ingredients into a small saucepan over gentle heat. Stir until well blended, but do not allow to boil.

Pour into a container. Cover when cold, and store in a refrigerator or cool place. It keeps for several weeks.

Caramel Syrup

> 20 *fluid oz caster sugar*   1 *pint boiling water*

Place the sugar in a large thick frying pan. Melt slowly over gentle heat, stirring constantly. Once melted, cook until the sugar is dark brown in colour.

Have the boiling water ready and pour it slowly over the sugar. Boil for a further 5-7 minutes, when the syrup should be the consistency of thin honey. Leave to cool slightly before pouring into screw-topped jars.

This syrup keeps indefinitely and has many uses, e.g.

in *Caramel Mousse* (p. 186) and *Caramel Ice Cream* (p. 191)

over *Ice Cream Sundaes* (pp. 193-5) and plain baked and steamed sponges.

Butterscotch Sauce

This we consider the best and most versatile of all sweet sauces. It is a universal favourite and keeps for months in a dry cool place, not necessarily a refrigerator.

3 *oz butter or margarine*	2 *fluid oz water*
2 *oz golden syrup*	1½ *oz plain flour*
5 *oz dark moist sugar*	¼ *pint milk*

Heat in a not too small saucepan the fat, syrup, sugar and water. Stir until sugar has dissolved. Then, without further stirring, allow to boil for three minutes. Remove from heat.

Slowly sieve the flour into the mixture. While stirring, gradually add the milk.

Replace over heat, and stir until it thickens.

Pour into a storage container, but do not cover until cold.

Some of the many ways of using Butterscotch Sauce:

> *with ice cream* (pp. 193–5)
> *served over, or cooked under baked and steamed sponge puddings* (pp. 170, 178)
> *as tartlet, pastry, and pancake fillings* (p. 73)
> *in apple fritters* (p. 22)
> *with cakes and biscuits* (pp. 144–167)

Once you have a supply of Butterscotch Sauce, you can use it in the suggested ways, in others of your own devising, or you can turn it into any of the Butterscotch Sauce variations. These do not keep as well as the plain sauce, so do not prepare too much at a time, not more than you expect to use in about two weeks.

BUTTERSCOTCH SAUCE VARIATIONS

Chocolate Sauce 2

This is an excellent sauce that is equally good served hot or cold. It can be reheated, baked or boiled, and is a winner when used as follows:

served over *Vanilla, Coffee or Chocolate Ice Creams* (pp. 193–5)
cooked with *Baked or Steamed Chocolate Sponge Puddings* (pp. 170, 178)
with *Pancakes* (p. 28)
mixed with *Water and Butter Icings* (pp. 165, 167)

Mix together:

1 *tablespoon cocoa*	2 *tablespoons Butterscotch Sauce*
3 *tablespoons boiling water*	

When cold, store in covered container in a refrigerator or cool place.

Coffee Sauce

Can be treated and used as given for *Chocolate Sauce* 2.

Mix together:

1 *teaspoon instant coffee*	2 *tablespoons Butterscotch Sauce*
2 *tablespoons boiling water*	

When cold, store in covered container in a refrigerator or cool place.

Spice Sauce

This is a nice sauce for *Pancakes* (p. 28) and *Spice Puddings* (pp. 170, 178) and is used in *Ginger Delights* (p. 195) and *Vanilla Sundaes* (pp. 193–4).

Mix together:

$\frac{1}{2}$ *teaspoon ground ginger*	2 *tablespoons boiling water*
$\frac{1}{8}$ *teaspoon cinnamon*	2 *tablespoons Butterscotch Sauce*
$\frac{1}{8}$ *teaspoon mixed spice*	

Orange Brandy Sauce

This is delicious for *Pancakes* (p. 28) and *orange flavoured baked or steamed Sponge Puddings* (pp. 170–8).

grated rind of 1 *orange,*	3 *tablespoons Butterscotch Sauce*
crushed with a little sugar	1$\frac{1}{2}$ *tablespoons brandy*
4 *tablespoons orange juice*	

Put all the ingredients in a small saucepan over gentle heat, and stir with a wooden spoon until blended.

HARD SAUCES

These are well worth the few minutes spent in their preparation. They keep for months, and without any further attention, emerge from the refrigerator as a delicious sauce for *steamed puddings, most baked sponges, apple and pastry dishes, and pancakes*. Made with lemon, they provide an inexpensive everyday sauce. Made with brandy, or a mixture of brandy and sherry, you have your *Brandy Butter* to serve with the Christmas pudding, and for any special occasion throughout the year.

Lemon, Brandy or Sherry Hard Sauce

¼ *lb fresh butter, warmed*	1 *tablespoon lemon juice, fresh*
¼ *lb caster sugar*	*or bottled,*
	or brandy or sherry

Beat the butter and sugar until light and creamy. Gradually add the chosen liquid. Beat well.

Store in a refrigerator container, or in a serving bowl covered with Look or foil.

Rum Butter

This is a very old recipe from the North. In bygone days, women did not grudge spending perhaps an hour beating a mixture, but now most of us would jib at such a task. Thus we suggest that a standard or hand electric mixer is used for this quite delicious hard sauce, unless you are prepared to beat it by hand for a very long time.

6 *oz soft brown sugar*	½ *teaspoon cinnamon*
2½ *fluid oz rum*	4 *oz melted butter*

Place sugar and cinnamon in the bowl of an electric mixer or a mixing bowl. Pour in the rum and stir. Add the butter, and mix well.

Now blend with the electric mixer, set at a high speed, until the mixture thickens and no longer shows signs of curdling.

Transfer the butter to a container and store in the refrigerator or a very cool place.

This, like the other hard sauces, is very good served with hot puddings. It also makes an excellent cake and biscuit filling (provided these are not too rich, for instance: *Orange Rum Chocolate Cake*, p. 149, and *Oatmeal Biscuits*, p. 162) and can be used in party flan and tartlet filling (p. 73).

FRUIT SYRUPS

These syrups show how a failure can turn into a triumph. When a batch of bramble jelly refused to set, it was used as a sauce. This proved so successful that when the supply came to an end, more fruit syrups had to be made. Hence the following recipes. They should keep for at least a year, are delicious, and can be used in so many ways. Here are a few examples: hot, with sponge puddings and pancakes; cold, with corn-flour moulds; cooked with apples in a very slow oven. The only draw-back for some people will be that a pressure cooker is necessary.

Bramble Syrup

2 *lbs sugar*   ½ *pint water*   2 *lbs blackberries*

Place sugar and water in a pressure cooker. Stir over heat until sugar has dissolved.

Put the food rack into the cooker and add the blackberries. Pressure-cook for 2 minutes at 15 lbs pressure. Reduce heat.

Stir the fruit into the juice, and pass the mixture through the finest disc of a Moulin-Legumes.

Return the sauce to the cooker and boil without the lid for 2 minutes. Pour into warm jars. Cover when cold.

Blackcurrant Syrup

1½ *lbs sugar*   1¼ *pints water*   1 *lb blackcurrants*

Prepare as for *Bramble Syrup*.

Raspberry Syrup

1 *lb sugar*   1 *lb raspberries*
8 *fluid oz water or*
½ *pint white wine or cheap sherry*

Prepare as for *Bramble Syrup*

Lemon or Orange Syrup

This syrup can be made with either fruit. Both are good, served hot or cold, and can be made throughout the year.

See also *Apple* and *Lemon* or *Orange Filling* (p. 75)

1 *lb lemons or oranges*   2 *pints water*
2 *tablespoons sugar*   2½ *lbs sugar*

Grate the rind, and crush it with 2 tablespoons sugar. Cover and set aside.

Soak the rindless fruit in water for 24 hours.

Next day, drain the fruit and cut it up. Put it, the grated rinds, and 2 pints fresh water in a pressure cooker. Cook for 1 hour at 15 lbs pressure. Reduce pressure.

Strain the fruit and pass it through the coarsest disc of a Moulin-Legumes. Return sieved fruit and the juice to the cooker. Add the sugar. Replace over heat, without the lid. Stir until the sugar has dissolved. Boil for 25 minutes.

Pour into warm jars. Cover when cold.

BASIC CREAM SAUCE

CREAM SAUCE AND ITS USES

Cream Sauce is the base of many dishes and sauces. It is, however, irritating to spend time fiddling around with a small quantity, when it is possible to make several days' supply in one operation.

This thick, buttery sauce will keep up to two weeks in a refrigerator. (Without a refrigerator it must not be made.) During that time, it will supply, as needed, the base for cream sauces, cream soups, soufflés, croquettes and other dishes.

Basic Cream Sauce

       ¼ *lb butter or margarine*   1 *pint milk*
       3 *oz plain flour*

Melt the butter or margarine in a saucepan. Remove from heat, and using a wooden spoon gradually stir in the flour. Cook gently for 1 minute, then remove from heat. Gradually add the milk, stirring continuously. When perfectly smooth, return to heat, and stir until the sauce thickens. Cook gently for a few minutes, stirring occasionally.

Pour most of the sauce into a container, leaving enough in the pan for immediate use.

We have found that the sauce keeps best in a plastic container with a close-fitting lid. This prevents a crust from forming and the sauce becoming dry. Do not seal or place in the refrigerator until quite cold.

Being so buttery, this basic cream sauce, though it emerges solid from the refrigerator, reheats easily. The desired flavours and additional liquids are then gradually added and stirred in with a wooden spoon.

Cream Sauce with Vegetables

This sauce is excellent with pressure-cooked vegetables, since so much of their goodness and flavour has gone into the 2½ to 5 oz of water in which they were cooked, and this goes into the sauce.

While the vegetables are cooking, heat some Cream Sauce slowly in a pan. When the vegetables are cooked, add enough of the liquid to make the sauce the desired consistency. This should also provide all the necessary flavour and seasoning.

Without a pressure cooker, the white sauce can be made by adding some of the water in which the vegetables were boiled to the heated Cream Sauce.

Cheese Sauce 2*

For *each heaped tablespoon Basic Cream Sauce* allow:

2 *tablespoons milk*	¼ *teaspoon made mustard*
1 *oz grated cheese*	*salt and pepper to taste*

Heat the Cream Sauce and milk gently in a saucepan, stirring until blended. Add the grated cheese, mustard and seasoning. Cook gently until the cheese has melted.

This sauce is delicious served over hard-boiled eggs and vegetables (see *Cauliflower au Gratin*, p. 15).

Curry Sauce

For *each heaped tablespoon Basic Cream Sauce* allow:

3 *tablespoons milk*	*a good pinch garlic powder*
2 *teaspoons curry powder*	⅛ *teaspoon salt*
1 *teaspoon black treacle*	¼ *teaspoon lemon juice (fresh or bottled)*

Heat the Cream Sauce and milk gently in a saucepan and stir until blended. Add remaining ingredients and simmer very gently for at least five minutes, stirring occasionally.

Serve over fish, hard boiled eggs, vegetables, or mixed with boiled rice or *Steamed Potatoes*, p. 114.

Tomato Sauce

For *each heaped tablespoon Basic Cream Sauce* allow:

3 *tablespoons milk*	1 *teaspoon sugar*
3 *teaspoons tomato purée*	¼ *teaspoon salt*
1 *teaspoon garlic vinegar*	*pepper to taste*

* *Cheese Sauce 1*, p. 7, is made with Cheese Foundation.

Heat the Cream Sauce and milk gently in a saucepan and stir until blended. Add the other ingredients and mix well.

Serve with eggs, boiled rice or pastas.

Mustard Sauce 2*

For *each heaped tablespoon of Basic Cream Sauce* allow:

2–3 tablespoons milk   *salt and pepper to taste*
1½ teaspoons French mustard

Heat the Cream Sauce, milk and mustard in a saucepan and stir well until smooth. Season.

Serve hot with herrings, mackerel, bacon and sausage dishes.

Caper Sauce

For *each heaped tablespoon of Basic Cream Sauce* allow:

2–3 tablespoons milk   *salt and pepper to taste*
½ tablespoon capers

Heat the Cream Sauce and the milk in a saucepan, stirring continuoulsy until smooth, then add the chopped capers.

Serve hot with boiled mutton, grilled herrings or mackerel.

Parsley Sauce

For *each heaped tablespoon of Basic Cream Sauce* allow:

2–3 tablespoons milk   *salt and pepper to taste*
½–1 tablespoon chopped parsley

Stir the Cream Sauce and milk in a small pan over low heat until blended and smooth. Add the chopped parsley and seasoning.

Serve hot with ham and fish dishes.

Egg Sauce

For *each heaped tablespoon of Basic Cream Sauce* allow:

2–3 tablespoons milk   *salt and pepper to taste*
1 hard boiled egg, sliced

Blend the Cream Sauce and milk in a small pan over low heat. Add the sliced hard boiled egg and seasoning.

Serve hot with veal and fish dishes.

* *Mustard Sauce 1*, is given on p. 76.

Hollandaise Sauce (Mock)

This is a foolproof version of the famous sauce. It is good served with asparagus, leeks, stewed celery, green vegetables, fish and eggs – poached, hard boiled, or en cocotte.

3 *heaped tablespoons Basic Cream Sauce* 1 *egg yolk*
2–3 *tablespoons milk* ¼ *oz butter*
Salt and pepper to taste 1 *tablespoon lemon juice,*
  fresh or bottled

Blend Cream Sauce and milk in a small saucepan over gentle heat. Add seasoning. Just before serving, beat the remaining ingredients into the hot sauce over a gentle heat until it thickens. If too thick, a little extra milk can be added.

Hot Sauce Tartare

For *each heaped tablespoon of Basic Cream Sauce* allow:
½–1 *tablespoon milk* 1 *teaspoon tarragon vinegar*
½ *tablespoon Mayonnaise* ¾ *tablespoon chopped pickles*
(any mayonnaise on ½ *tablespoon grated onion* (optional)
pp. 98–9) ¼ *teaspoon dry or made mustard*
1 *teaspoon chopped parsley,*
fresh or dried

Heat Cream Sauce in a small pan over gentle heat. Stir in the milk. Mix well before adding the remaining ingredients.
See also *Sauce Tartare* (p. 100).

Horseradish Sauce 2*

To serve 4 allow:
2 *heaped tablespoons Basic Cream Sauce* ½ *teaspoon sugar*
2 *tablespoons milk* *Salt and pepper*
1 *tablespoon grated horseradish*
or 1 *dessertspoon Heinz Dried Horseradish,*
  soaked in milk

Blend the Cream Sauce and milk over low heat until smooth. Stir in the horseradish and sugar. Season to taste.
Serve hot or cold, or cook in *Sliced Meat Fritters* (p. 19).

* *Horseradish Sauce 1*, is given on p. 77.

Cucumber Sauce

To serve 4 allow:

2 *heaped tablespoons Basic Cream Sauce*   3 *tablespoons peeled,*
2 *tablespoons milk*   *grated cucumber*
                                                  Salt and freshly ground
                                                  pepper

Blend the Cream Sauce and milk over low heat until smooth. Stir in the grated cucumber and seasoning.
Serve hot with fish dishes.

White Chaud Froid Sauce

To coat a whole chicken allow:

1 *tablespoon gelatine*   ½ *pint Single Cream* (pp. 105–6)
4 *tablespoons cold water*   *salt and pepper to taste*
5 *heaped tablespoons Basic Cream Sauce*

Soak the gelatine in the cold water for 5 minutes.
Put the Cream Sauce in a saucepan and bring to boil. Add the gelatine and stir until dissolved. Add cream and seasoning.
Strain through a fine sieve and leave to cool. Pour over cold cooked chicken just as it is beginning to set.

Orange Sauce

This is a delicious quick sweet sauce to serve with hot sponge puddings and ice creams.

To serve 4 allow:

2 *heaped tablespoons Basic Cream Sauce*   4 *tablespoons orange squash*

Heat the Cream Sauce in a small saucepan, then gradually stir in the orange squash.

Lemon Sauce

To serve 4 allow:

2 *heaped tablespoons Basic Cream Sauce*   2 *tablespoons unsweetened*
2 *tablespoons milk*   *lemon juice*
                                                  2 *tablespoons caster sugar*

Blend the Cream Sauce and milk over low heat until smooth. Stir in the caster sugar and lemon juice.
Serve hot with steamed and baked puddings.

Brandy Sauce

To serve 4 allow:

2 *heaped tablespoons Basic Cream Sauce* 1 *tablespoon caster sugar*
3 *tablespoons milk* 1–2 *tablespoons brandy*

Blend Cream Sauce and milk over low heat until smooth. Stir in the sugar and brandy.
Serve hot with Christmas pudding.

Jam or Marmalade Sauce

To serve 4 allow:

1 *heaped tablespoon Basic Cream Sauce* 4 *tablespoons jam or*
1 *dessertspoon caster sugar* *marmalade*
  1 *teaspoon lemon juice*

Heat the Cream Sauce in a saucepan and add the sugar, jam or marmalade, and lemon juice. Mix well and serve hot with baked and steamed puddings.

EMERGENCY SOUPS

Basic Cream Sauce is the foundation of the following recipes, which are inexpensive and made in a moment.

Cream of Tomato Soup

To serve 2 allow:

2 *heaped tablespoons Basic Cream Sauce* 2 *fluid oz milk*
3 *teaspoons tomato purée* *pinch of garlic powder*
½ *chicken stock cube* dissolved in (optional)
½ *pint boiling water* *pepper to taste*

Warm in a saucepan over low heat the Cream Sauce and tomato purée and mix well together. Gradually stir in the chicken stock and milk. Season with garlic powder and pepper. Serve.

Cream of Chicken Soup

To serve 3–4 allow:

3 *heaped tablespoons Basic Cream Sauce* pinch of garlic powder
1 *chicken stock cube* dissolved in (optional)
¾ *pint boiling water*

Warm the Cream Sauce. Gradually stir in the chicken stock. Serve.

C.A.—D

SOUFFLÉS

Soufflés are made most successfully with Cream Sauce.

The initial stages can be prepared in advance, except for the beating and folding in of the egg whites, which must be done immediately before the soufflé is put in the oven.

Use a 2 pint straight-sided dish. Leave ungreased, as this helps the soufflé to stick to the sides of the dish and so rise further.

Bake in the centre of a moderate oven, 375°F, Mark 5, for 20–30 minutes, according to the size of the dish. Remember, keep the oven door firmly closed until the given time is up and serve immediately.

Prawn or Shrimp Soufflé   Oven Setting 375°F, Mark 5

To serve 4 allow:

5 *heaped tablespoons Basic Cream Sauce*	2 *teaspoons anchovy essence*
¼ *pint shelled prawns or shrimps,*	3 *egg yolks*
fresh, frozen or tinned	3 *egg whites*
1 *teaspoon lemon juice*	

Heat the Cream Sauce in a saucepan until boiling, then remove from heat. Cut the prawn flesh into small pieces, and add to the sauce with the lemon juice and anchovy essence. Stir in the yolks one at a time. Return to the heat for a minute to allow the yolks to thicken, stirring constantly. Cool slightly before folding in the stiffly beaten egg whites.

Transfer to an ungreased 2 pint soufflé dish, and bake in the centre of a pre-heated oven for 30 minutes.

Ham Soufflé   Oven Setting 375°F, Mark 5

To serve 4 allow:

5 *heaped tablespoons Basic Cream Sauce*	3 *egg yolks*
4–6 *oz minced ham*	3 *egg whites*
1 *teaspoon made mustard*	

Heat the Cream Sauce in a saucepan until boiling. Remove from heat and stir in the minced ham and mustard, then beat in the egg yolks one at a time. Return to the heat and, stirring constantly, cook for a further minute to allow the yolks to thicken. Cool slightly before folding in the stiffly beaten egg whites.

Transfer to an ungreased 2 pint soufflé dish, and bake in the centre of a pre-heated oven for 30 minutes.

Mushroom Soufflé   Oven Setting 375°F, Mark 5

To serve 4 allow:

½ lb mushrooms	salt and pepper
2 oz butter	3 egg yolks
5 heaped tablespoons Basic Cream Sauce	3 egg whites

Prepare the mushrooms by dipping them in boiling water for a second and then wiping them dry with kitchen paper. Slice finely, then sauté gently in the butter for about 5 minutes.

Heat the Cream Sauce in a saucepan, then add the mushrooms, seasoning, and egg yolks one at a time.

Bring the mixture back to boiling point and cook gently for a further minute, to allow the yolks to thicken. Cool slightly before folding in the stiffly beaten egg whites.

Transfer to an ungreased 2 pint soufflé dish and bake in the centre of a pre-heated oven for 30 minutes.

Cheese Soufflé   Oven Setting 375°F, Mark 5

To serve 4 allow:

5 heaped tablespoons Basic Cream Sauce	3 egg yolks
3 oz grated cheese (including parmesan)	3 egg whites
Pinch of salt, pepper and mustard	

Heat the Cream Sauce until boiling. Add the cheese and seasoning, stir and simmer until the cheese is melted. Remove from heat and beat in egg yolks one at a time.

Return to stove for a further minute to permit the yolks to thicken. Allow to cool slightly before adding the stiffly beaten egg whites.

Pour into an ungreased 2 pint soufflé dish, or four small individual dishes, and cook in a pre-heated oven for 20–30 minutes, depending on size.

Chocolate Soufflé   Oven Setting 375°F, Mark 5

To serve 4 allow:

5 heaped tablespoons Basic Cream Sauce	4 egg yolks
4 oz grated plain chocolate	4 egg whites
2 oz caster sugar	a little icing sugar

Heat the Cream Sauce and the grated chocolate together in a pan over a low heat until the chocolate is melted, stirring constantly. Remove from heat and beat in the sugar and egg yolks, one at a time.

Return to heat and cook for a further minute to allow the yolks to thicken. Leave to cool slightly before folding in the stiffly beaten egg whites.

Pour mixture into an ungreased 2 pint soufflé dish and bake in the centre of a pre-heated oven for 30 minutes.

Dust with sifted icing sugar and serve with cream.

Soufflé aux Liqueurs   Oven Setting 375°F, Mark 5

To serve 4 allow:

5 *heaped tablespoons Basic Cream Sauce*	4 *egg yolks*
3 *oz caster sugar*	4 *egg whites*
2 *tablespoons any liqueur*	*a little icing sugar*

Heat the Cream Sauce in a saucepan until boiling. Remove from heat, and beat in the sugar and the egg yolks, one at a time. Return to the heat and, stirring constantly, cook for a further minute to allow the yolks to thicken. Add the liqueur, and cool slightly before folding in the stiffly beaten egg whites.

Transfer to an ungreased 2 pint soufflé dish and bake in the centre of a pre-heated oven for 30 minutes.

Dust with icing sugar and serve.

CROQUETTES

These can be made quickly and easily with Basic Cream Sauce. They can either be made with fresh ingredients, or with left-over cooked meat or fish. This should be minced or shredded, according to preference, together with a little onion if liked. Two parts cooked food to one part cold Basic Cream Sauce gives a good consistency.

Although croquettes are usually egg and breadcrumbed before being deep fried, they can, if preferred, be dipped in thin Coating Batter and treated as *Fritters* (p. 22).

Croquettes from Left-overs

To serve 4 allow:

4 *heaped tablespoons cold Basic Cream Sauce*	*seasoning*
8 *heaped tablespoons minced or shredded cooked*	1 *beaten egg*
food	*breadcrumbs*
a little minced onion (optional)	

Blend Cream Sauce, cooked food, and seasoning in a mixing bowl. Shape into croquettes (small fat sausages). Dip in the beaten egg and roll in the breadcrumbs.

Fry in deep, very hot fat until golden brown. Drain on absorbent paper and serve immediately.

Cheese Croquettes

To serve 4 allow:

4 *heaped tablespoons Basic Cream Sauce*	*salt and pepper to taste*
8 *heaped tablespoons grated cheese*	*beaten egg*
½ *teaspoon Worcester sauce*	*breadcrumbs*

Blend the Cream Sauce and the grated cheese in a mixing bowl. Add the Worcester sauce and the seasoning. Mix well.

Form into croquettes (this quantity makes about 12). Dip in beaten egg and roll in breadcrumbs.

Fry in deep, very hot fat for a few minutes until they are golden brown. Drain on absorbent paper and serve.

Salmon or Tuna Fish Croquettes

To serve 4 allow:

6½–7 *oz tin of salmon or tuna*	1 *teaspoon chopped parsley*
4 *heaped tablespoons Basic Cream Sauce*	*beaten egg*
1 *teaspoon lemon juice* (fresh or bottled)	*breadcrumbs*
seasoning	*slices of lemon*

Mix the fish, Cream Sauce, lemon juice, seasoning and parsley well together in a mixing bowl. Shape into croquettes. Dip in beaten egg and roll in breadcrumbs.

Fry in deep, very hot fat until golden brown.

Drain on absorbent paper and serve garnished with parsley and slices of lemon.

Mushroom and Hard Boiled Egg Croquettes

To serve 4 allow:

6 *diced hard boiled eggs*	*seasoning*
5 *oz mushrooms, cleaned* (p. 91), *sliced and cooked in a little butter*	*beaten egg*
	breadcrumbs
5 *heaped tablespoons Basic Cream Sauce*	*parsley*

Mix hard boiled eggs, mushrooms, Cream Sauce and seasoning well together. Shape into croquettes. Dip in beaten egg, then roll in bread-crumbs.

Fry in deep, very hot fat until golden brown.

Drain on absorbent paper and serve hot, garnished with fresh or fried parsley.

Croquettes wrapped in Bacon

Both the above and the *Cheese Croquettes* are delicious with strips of thinly sliced bacon wrapped round each before they are egg and breadcrumbed.

Beurrek Croquettes (see *Beurrek Filling*, pp. 68–9)

OTHER CREAM SAUCE RECIPES

Fish Cooked in Cream Sauce   Oven Setting 425°F, Mark 7
                                                   or lowest possible

All fish, from huss to turbot, is good cooked this way. When choosing fish fillets, try to get the fishmonger to skin them – if not, skin them yourself and remove any bones; these are difficult to find once the fish is cooked.

Place the fish in a casserole on top of the following:

Basic Cream Sauce, about 1½ heaped   *a little anchovy essence or*
*   tablespoons per serving*   *   tarragon vinegar* (optional)
chopped parsley or fennel   *sliced hard boiled egg*
salt and pepper to taste   *   (optional)*
                                              capers (optional)

When using the hot oven, stand covered casserole in a meat tin containing an inch of cold water, and bake for 20–30 minutes.

When using the cool oven, slip the casserole – uncovered – into a brown paper bag and cook for 1½–2 hours.

Carefully lift the cooked fish on to a warm dish. Stir the fish juices into the sauce, and pour over the fish. Serve.

Fish Pie

This is cooked as for *Fish Cooked in Cream Sauce*. After lifting the cooked fish, remove any lurking skin and bones. Flaké it and return to the well stirred sauce. Top with *Creamed Potatoes* (p. 115). This dish can either be browned in the oven or under the grill and served, or cooled, stored and reheated and browned as required.

Fish Cakes

We challenge anyone to find an easier way of producing fish cakes, and such good ones into the bargain.

They are prepared as for *Fish Pie*, except that instead of topping with *Creamed Potato*, plain *mashed potato* is beaten into the flaked fish and sauce with a fork. Allow enough potato to make the mixture just manageable, but not stiff.

Put *brown breadcrumbs* into a small round basin. Divide the fish mixture into the number of fish cakes required. Drop these sections, one at a time, into the crumbs. Shake the basin so that the fish cakes bounce round and round, thus becoming circular and crumb-covered. Flatten cakes slightly and put them on to a plate.

Store in a refrigerator or a cool place until required: then fry. They should not be fried until they are cold and firm.

Creamed Green Vegetables

Finely chop, mince, sieve or liquidize *strained, freshly cooked vegetables*. Return them to the pan in which they were cooked. Mix *Basic Cream Sauce* in with a fork (amount according to taste). Add *salt* and *pepper* and to *spinach* a little *sugar*. Reheat gently.

Baked Cabbage   Oven Setting 350°F, Mark 4

To serve 4 allow:
a medium sized cabbage
5 heaped tablespoons Basic Cream Sauce
3 tablespoons milk

3–4 tablespoons grated
  cheese (more if liked)
about ½ oz butter
breadcrumbs

Boil cabbage until tender. Chop it coarsely.

Heat the Cream Sauce in a small saucepan and stir in the milk.

Grease an oven dish liberally with about half of the butter, and place in it a third of the cabbage. Cover with a third of the Sauce and sprinkle on a third of the cheese. Add another two layers of cabbage, sauce and cheese. Press them well down, and top with breadcrumbs, and dots of the remaining butter.

Bake in pre-heated oven for about 30 minutes.

Any vegetable left-overs can be cooked this way. Mixed vegetables make a savoury dish.

Onions au Gruyère

To serve 4 allow:

8 *medium-sized onions*   4 *oz grated Gruyère,*
4 *heaped tablespoons Basic Cream Sauce*   *Emmenthal or Jarlsberg*

Boil onions until tender. While they are cooking, heat the Cream Sauce in a saucepan, thin slightly with some of the onion water, then stir in the grated cheese.

Drain onions, transfer to vegetable dish, and pour over the sauce. Serve.

This delicious sauce can be used on other vegetables.

Cauliflower au Gratin

This is cooked as given on p. 15, except *Cheese Sauce* 2 is used instead of *Cheese Sauce* 1.

Scalloped Potatoes and Bacon (see p. 119)

Macaroni Cheese 2*   Oven Setting 425°F, Mark 7

To serve 2–3 allow:

3 *oz macaroni*   *a little milk*
4 *heaped tablespoons Basic Cream Sauce*   *breadcrumbs*
1 *teaspoon made mustard*   *a little butter or margarine*
2–3 *oz grated cheese, strong,*
     including if possible a little parmesan

Cook the macaroni in about 2 pints of well salted boiling water until tender (15–20 minutes). While this is cooking, heat the Cream Sauce in a flame-proof dish or a saucepan. Add the mustard, most of the cheese and a little milk – not too much. Mix well. When using a saucepan, transfer mixture to a greased oven dish. Top with breadcrumbs, the remaining cheese, and dot with butter or margarine.

Bake in pre-heated oven for about 20 minutes, or, if to be served immediately, brown under a hot grill.

* *Macaroni Cheese 1*, p. 10, is made with Cheese Foundation.

Macaroni Cheese with Frankfurters and Sausages
and
Macaroni Cheese and Eggs
and
Macaroni Cheese with Eggs and Frankfurters or Sausages
and
Macaroni Cheese and Left-overs

These four dishes can be made with *Macaroni Cheese* 2 in the same way
as given for *Macaroni Cheese* 1 on p. 10.

Croque Monsieur 2*

For each portion allow: .

2–3 *heaped tablespoons Basic Cream Sauce*	1 *or* 2 *thick slices of cooked*
1 *oz grated cheese*	*ham*
2 *slices bread, crusts removed*	*a little French mustard*
	(optional)
	a little parsley

Heat the Cream Sauce in a small pan. Add the cheese and stir until
blended. Spread one side of each piece of bread with this mixture, and
make a sandwich with the ham and mustard as the filling. Fry in plenty
of hot lard or dripping or, if preferred, toast each side under the grill.
Garnish with fried parsley.

Croque Monsieur can also be made with *corned beef* or *luncheon
meat*.

Beurrek Filling (pp. 68–9)

MAYONNAISE *and* SALAD DRESSINGS

A must for most households – hence the thousands of manufactured
mayonnaises and salad dressings sold every day. These cannot be compared with the real mayonnaise and delicious dressings one can make
for oneself, which don't take long to prepare and keep for months.

MAYONNAISE

Mayonnaise, it is said, was discovered by Cardinal Richlieu early in the
seventeenth century. It has remained popular ever since, to be used for
fish (hot or cold, e.g. salmon), poultry, meat, vegetables and salads.

* *Croque Monsieur 1*, pp. 11–12, is made with Cheese Foundation.

A true mayonnaise should contain no less than 50 per cent oil, but may curdle if more than ½ pint is used with 2 egg yolks.

Be sure all the ingredients are room temperature
Never use eggs straight out of the refrigerator

Mayonnaise should be stored in a cool place and not in a refrigerator.

Mayonnaise 1

2 *egg yolks, room temperature*	2 *tablespoons vinegar or lemon juice*
½ *teaspoon salt*	(*fresh or bottled*)
½ *teaspoon dry mustard*	½ *pint olive or salad oil*
a little pepper	*sugar to taste* (optional)

Rinse mixing bowl in hot water, dry thoroughly, and stand it on a cloth wrung out in very hot water (this steadies the bowl). Put in the yolks, salt, mustard, pepper and a few drops of the vinegar or lemon juice. Mix well.

Measure 2 fluid oz of the ½ pint of oil into a small measure with a spout, or a small jug. Beating vigorously with a wooden spoon, add a few drops of the oil to the egg mixture, and continue adding a few drops at a time, still beating, until the 2 fluid oz are incorporated. Now, without relaxing the beating, the remaining oil can be added in a thin continuous stream. The rest of the vinegar or lemon juice is now added and, should the mayonnaise be considered too thick, a little boiling water can also be included. Lastly, if a sweet mayonnaise is preferred, though this is unorthodox, add sugar to taste.

Mayonnaise 2

This also is a true mayonnaise, excellent, and wonderfully quick to produce. The only snag is that an electric blender is essential.

2 *egg yolks, room temperature*	2 *level teaspoons caster sugar*
½ *teaspoon each salt and mustard*	(optional)
½ *level teaspoon ground pepper*	½ *pint olive oil*
1 *tablespoon wine vinegar*	1 *tablespoon lemon juice*
	1 *tablespoon boiling water*

Place egg yolks, seasonings, vinegar and sugar into the blender. Using lowest speed, just blend them together. Remove the centre cap in the blender top and pour the oil slowly on to the egg yolks, still using lowest speed. Add the lemon juice, and lastly the boiling water.

Mayonnaise Sauce

This is good, easy to make, not too rich, and makes a grand substitute for true mayonnaise.

4 *egg yolks*	2 *tablespoons tarragon vinegar*
½ *teaspoon salt*	2 *tablespoons lemon juice, fresh or*
¼ *teaspoon freshly ground pepper*	*bottled*
1 *teaspoon sugar, more or less*	3 *tablespoons warm water*
to taste	½ *small onion, grated, or* 1 *teaspoon*
4 *tablespoons olive oil*	*fresh or* ½ *teaspoon dried chervil*

Put the egg yolks into a small saucepan and add all the other ingredients. Stir with a wooden spoon until well blended.

Place pan over medium heat and now whisk the mixture with a rotary whisk until the mayonnaise boils and thickens. Remove from heat and stir with the wooden spoon again for a minute.

Pour the sauce into a jar. Cover when cold.

Mayonnaise Sauce can be stored in a refrigerator and can be reheated.

Canadian Mayonnaise

This is thinner than true mayonnaise, otherwise a good substitute. It is not nearly so rich, far cheaper, and fun to make.

2 *egg yolks*	4 *fluid oz salad oil*
1 *teaspoon salt*	4 *fluid oz vinegar or lemon juice,*
¼ *teaspoon pepper*	*fresh or bottled*
1 *teaspoon mustard*	(The mayonnaise keeps longer when
1 *tablespoon sugar* (optional –	made with vinegar)
children like considerably	1 *oz margarine*
more)	2 *tablespoons plain flour*
	8 *fluid oz warm water*

Put yolks, seasoning, sugar, oil, vinegar or lemon juice into a mixing bowl. Do not stir.

Melt margarine in saucepan.

Remove from heat. Stir in the flour and slowly add the warm water.

When smooth, replace over heat, and stir until the mixture thickens and boils.

Pour the hot sauce immediately on to the ingredients in the mixing bowl, and, using a rotary whisk, whisk the whole lot together vigorously. Then, in a matter of moments, the bowl will contain a lovely creamy mayonnaise.

Pour into a container and cover when cold. Store in a refrigerator or a cool place.

This mayonnaise can be heated up to simmering point, but must not boil. It is therefore safer to reheat it in a double saucepan or in a basin over hot water.

SAUCES MADE FROM MAYONNAISE

Except for *Green Sauce*, these can be made with any of the four previous recipes, but if a hot sauce is required, use only *Mayonnaise Sauce* or *Canadian Mayonnaise*.

Sauce Tartare

Blend the following:

1 *dessertspoon finely chopped gherkins or capers*	1 *dessertspoon finely chopped chives* (optional)
1 *tablespoon chopped parsley*	1 *teaspoon made mustard*
	¼ *pint mayonnaise*

See *Hot Sauce Tartare*, p. 87.

Sauce Niçoise

This sauce is good with fish and shellfish.

Blend the following:

1 *tablespoon tomato purée*	1 *teaspoon chopped chives* (optional)
1 *tablespoon chopped pepper or gherkin*	¼ *pint mayonnaise*
1 *teaspoon chopped parsley*	

Green Sauce

Make this sauce with *Mayonnaise* 1 or 2. It looks attractive, and is good with cold salmon, lobster, or other fish.

4 *sprigs of watercress*	2 *sprigs of parsley*
4 *leaves of spinach*	¼ *pint Mayonnaise*

Wash watercress, spinach and parsley thoroughly, and cover with boiling water. Let stand for 5 or 6 minutes. Drain, put into cold water, and drain again, squeezing out all the surplus moisture.

Pass through the medium disc of a Moulin Legumes or liquidize the wilted greens. Mix well with the mayonnaise. Add extra seasoning if wished.

Horseradish Sauce 1, p. 77

Mayonnaise Chaud Froid

This is good for coating fish or lobster before they are garnished.

1 *dessertspoon powdered gelatine*   8 *fluid oz Mayonnaise*
1 *fluid oz cold water*

Place the gelatine in a pudding basin and add the water. Set basin over a pan of boiling water and steam until the gelatine is thoroughly dissolved. Fold in the mayonnaise, mix well, and use before the sauce begins to set.

FRENCH DRESSINGS OR VINAIGRETTES

Classic French Dressing

Used for tossed green salads, hors d'oeuvres and marinating salad mixtures.

Make it in a pint screw-topped jar. Before using, shake well until all the ingredients are blended.

It keeps for some time in a refrigerator or a cool place.

Pour into the jar:

6 *fluid oz salad oil*   1 *teaspoon Worcester sauce (optional)*
2 *fluid oz vinegar or lemon juice* $\frac{1}{3}$–1 *teaspoon salt*
  (*fresh or bottled*) $\frac{1}{2}$ *teaspoon paprika (optional)*
1–3 *teaspoons sugar* $\frac{1}{4}$ *teaspoon freshly ground pepper*
1 *clove garlic cut in half*

Vinaigrette with Fine Herbs

Used for tossed green salads, hors d'oeuvres and cold fish.

Mix together:

4 *tablespoons French Dressing*   1 *tablespoon mixed chopped parsley*
1 *teaspoon made mustard*   *tarragon, chervil and chives*

Vinaigrette for Hors d'oeuvres

Mix together:

4 tablespoons French Dressing
1 tablespoon vinegar or lemon
 juice
1 teaspoon chopped capers

1 teaspoon each chopped parsley,
 tarragon, chervil and chives
1 tablespoon chopped hard boiled egg

Diet Dressing

Those who are slimming may prefer this to French Dressing.

Mix together in a pint screw-topped jar:

¼ pint salad oil
2½ fluid oz lemon juice,
 fresh or bottled
2½ fluid oz water
¼ teaspoon salt

2½ fluid oz ketchup
1 teaspoon dry mustard
¼ teaspoon paprika
½ teaspoon Worcester sauce

Shake well before using.

Sour Cream Salad Dressings, p. 109

SALADS

Potato Salad

potatoes   salt, pepper, paprika
French Dressing   Mayonnaise

Boil, steam or pressure-cook potatoes in their skins. When tender but not too soft, strain. Peel and slice as soon as they are cool enough to handle, and then marinate for an hour in French Dressing.

Add, and carefully mix in, plenty of Mayonnaise.

Potato and Celery Salad

Make as for *Potato Salad*, but include *a large cup of thinly cut celery.*

Cucumber Mayonnaise

This is a delicious accompaniment to fried or grilled fish or meat.

3 tablespoons grated peeled cucumber
2 tablespoons Mayonnaise
a little salt and freshly milled pepper

Mix all the ingredients well together and serve.

Winter Salad

head of celery	*watercress*
1 *small onion*	*beetroot*
Mayonnaise	*hard boiled eggs*

Shred or grate celery and onion and mix with Mayonnaise.

Arrange in a circle on a shallow dish. Stand watercress upright in the centre. Place beetroot cut in rounds all round the edge alternately with quarters of hard-boiled eggs.

FISH AND MAYONNAISE DISHES

Salmon Mayonnaise   Oven Settings 425°F, Mark 7
                                              or lowest possible

Salmon and mayonnaise are recognized as perfect partners, so why not cook the salmon in a mayonnaise, so that the fish juices can blend in with the sauce? It can be served hot or cold. This is not advised for fresh Scotch Salmon, but is excellent for chilled or frozen fish.

Use:

cuts of chilled salmon, or frozen salmon steaks
Canadian Mayonnaise or *Mayonnaise Sauce*
Cucumber (optional)

If frozen salmon is used, thaw out before cooking.

Place fish in a casserole. Spoon the mayonnaise round it, allowing about 2 tablespoons per serving. When fish is to be eaten hot, cover it with thin slices of cucumber.

When using the hot oven, stand covered casserole in a meat tin containing an inch of cold water and bake for 20–30 minutes.

When using the cool oven, slip the uncovered casserole into a brown paper bag and cook for $1\frac{1}{2}$–2 hours.

Carefully lift cooked fish and cucumber (when used) on to a dish.

Remove skin and bones from cuts and steaks. The cuts can either be divided into portions or flaked.

Mix the fish juices in the casserole with the mayonnaise. Return fish to casserole.

If to be served hot, decorate with the cucumber and reheat fish in covered dish just long enough to regain the correct temperature.

If to be served cold, leave the fish uncovered until cold.

Store in refrigerator or cool place until required. Serve with lettuce and finely sliced cucumber.

Fish Salad

This is prepared as for *Salmon Mayonnaise.*

Use:

any not too bony fish (fillets of the larger, coarser fish are quite satisfactory)	*shrimps or prawns can be added to the Canadian Mayonnaise or Mayonnaise Sauce*

Serve with a good salad which includes sliced hard-boiled egg.

Fish Grilled with Mayonnaise

For each portion allow:

a fish steak or a piece of fish fillet, skinned	*1 tablespoon Canadian Mayonnaise*
salt and pepper to taste	*or Mayonnaise Sauce*
1 teaspoon salad oil	*a little flour*

Grease grid and light grill.

Sprinkle fish with salt and pepper, and brush with salad oil. Place on hot grid and grill for about 5 minutes, or until brown. Turn fish carefully. Spread the uncooked side evenly with the mayonnaise and sprinkle with a little flour.

Grill for a further 5 to 10 minutes, possibly longer for cutlets, until tender and brown.

CREAM, CHEESE *and* CUSTARD

Any household, large or small, possessing a liquidizer or a cream-making machine, can always enjoy delicious cream and cream cheese with very little effort or expense.

CREAMS

An adequate and constant supply of cream is appreciated by most cooks, as this helps to transform mundane dishes into haute cuisine.

Whipping Cream

*¼ pint top milk   1½ oz to 2 oz salt-free butter, according to richness of
top of milk*

By pouring off 1 to 2 inches of top milk from each bottle as it is un-
sealed, ¼ pint is quickly accumulated. Of course large families with a
large milk consumption will collect more top milk, and will also need
more cream. Fortunately the quantity of cream that can be made always
seems to meet the demand. A good plan is to pour off your top milk into
a small, covered, refrigerator container which you have marked at the
¼ pint–7½ fluid oz or ½ pint level, according to your needs. You will then
know at a glance just how much you have collected to date.

Put the top milk with the butter in a small pan over heat and allow
to boil. Liquidize the hot mixture for not more than 30 seconds, or
pump it through a cream-making machine. Chill for about 12 hours.
The cream will now whip up quickly and will keep for several days in a
refrigerator.

Cream Garnish, p. 109

Single Cream

When single cream is wanted, there is no need to dissipate top milk: use
full cream milk.

First boil, then liquidize or pump through a cream-making machine:

*¼ pint milk   2½ oz butter, salted or salt-free,
                according to savoury or sweet use for cream*

This cream will not whip up, but can be used immediately.

Sour Cream

Sour cream is found in many recipes: a few are given here. It can be
made with whipping cream or single cream, provided they are dead cold.
Only use whipping cream when you have no available single cream, or
want an extra thick sour cream.

SMALL QUANTITY

1 tablespoon cream   ¼ teaspoon bottled lemon juice

LARGER QUANTITY

¼ *pint cream*   1 *dessertspoon bottled lemon juice*

A FEW CREAM RECIPES

Omelette à la Crême (A soufflé omelette)

To serve 2 allow:

3 *eggs*   *salt and pepper*
1½ *tablespoons Single Cream*   ½ *oz butter*

Separate 2 of the eggs. With a rotary whisk, whisk the whites stiffly. With a fork, work in the yolks and the remaining egg, unbeaten, and then the cream. Season to taste.

Heat a frying pan, preferably a non-stick or one reserved for omelettes: failing that, see p. 8. Put the butter in the pan, and when it is hot but not brown, pour in the mixture. When golden, fold it over, transfer to a hot dish, and serve immediately.

Egg Mousse 1 (Egg Mousse 2, p. 183)

To serve 6 allow:

6 *hard boiled eggs,* sliced   ½ *pint whipping cream*
10 *oz tin consommé soup*   *salt and pepper to taste*

Blend the sliced eggs with the consommé soup, either in an electrie blender or through a fine sieve.

Whip the cream until thick.

Fold in the egg mixture and seasoning. Transfer to a serving bowl and chill well in a refrigerator.

Before serving, decorate with *slices of tomato and cucumber*.

Eggs en Cocotte   Oven Setting 375°F, Mark 5

For this French way of cooking eggs, you need the little individual earthenware dishes, usually with a handle, that can be bought almost anywhere in this country.

Allow for *each egg:*

1 *tablespoon cream*   *a pinch of salt*
2 *saltspoons butter*   *boiling water*

Put the cocotte dishes in the oven for a few moments to heat.

Pour the cream into each dish and return to the oven for a further 2 minutes, or until the cream is quite hot, but not boiling.

Break the eggs carefully into the cream, add the butter and salt.

Put the cocottes into a deep meat tin or any suitable container. Pour in sufficient boiling water to reach halfway up the dishes. Cover the container with a dish or lid and place in the heated oven, where the water will be kept simmering without boiling.

Cook for 6 to 7 minutes, till the eggs are of the consistency of a lightly poached egg.

Dry the cocotte dishes and serve immediately.

These can be served with *Buck Rarebit* (p. 9).

Hot Slaw

An old American recipe.

To serve 3 or 4 allow:

a young white cabbage	*salt and pepper to taste*
1 *oz butter*	1 *egg, well beaten*
2 *or 3 tablespoons boiling water*	¼ *pint Sour Cream*

Cut cabbage into quarters after removing outer leaves. Cut out the core and shred the remainder as finely as possible.

Melt the butter in a frying pan, add the boiling water and put in the cabbage. Season. Cover pan and cook very gently until the cabbage is quite tender.

Now add the egg and continue to cook, stirring continuously, for three or four minutes.

Lastly add the cream. Leave over heat until once again thoroughly hot. Serve at once. Intended as a hot dish; it is also good eaten cold.

Potato and Cheese Moulds, p. 124

Russian Potatoes, p. 127

Hungarian Egg and Potato Pie, p. 128

Baked Herring Potatoes, pp. 129–130

Mushrooms Baked in Sour Cream   Oven Setting 350°F, Mark 4

A nice Austrian recipe.

To serve 3–4 allow:

½ *lb mushrooms, cleaned* (p. 91)	*salt and pepper to taste*
1 *tablespoon chopped parsley*	¼ *pint Sour Cream*
2 *tablespoons grated onion*	

Place the mushrooms, parsley, onion and seasoning in a well buttered oven dish with a lid. Cover with the cream.

Bake in pre-heated oven for 25 to 30 minutes. Serve.

Vegetable Marrow Cooked in Sour Cream

This delicious way of cooking very young marrows or courgettes comes from Hungary.

For 1 *or* 2 *young marrows* allow:

salt	1½ *teaspoons flour*
butter or lard	½ *pint Sour Cream*
1 *teaspoon paprika*	

Peel the marrow or courgettes, cut into thin, narrow slices and freely sprinkle with salt. Leave for an hour or longer to dehydrate. Strain, and dry with a cloth or kitchen paper.

Put a little fat in a pan, and when hot, cook the vegetable, sprinkled with the paprika, without browning, for 5 minutes. Stir in the flour, then the cream, cover pan and simmer gently for 8 to 10 minutes. Serve.

Mustard Cream

This is good served with cold chicken, fish or shellfish.

1 *teaspoon made mustard*	a *few drops of lemon juice*
a *little salt*	¼ *pint Whipping Cream*

Add the salt and lemon to the mustard. Stir in the cream. This can be whipped or not according to preference.

Horseradish Cream

Add *Whipped Cream* to *freshly grated or bottled horseradish.*

Sour Cream Sauce

½ *oz butter or margarine*	1 *teaspoon sugar*
2 *tablespoons minced onion*	¾ *teaspoon salt*
1 *tablespoon plain flour*	6 *fluid oz Sour Cream*
a *pinch of paprika*	1 *teaspoon vinegar*

Heat the fat in the top of a double saucepan, and brown the onion. Add flour, paprika, sugar and salt and cook for about one minute.

Remove from heat. Stir in the cream and cook over boiling water until the sauce thickens. Add the vinegar.

Serve hot with vegetables or fish.

Sour-Sweet Cream Sauce

This is nice mixed with vegetables, especially with broad, French and runner beans.

1 *beaten egg*	3 *tablespoons vinegar*
¼ *pint Sour Cream*	¼ *teaspoon paprika*
3 *tablespoons sugar*	½ *teaspoon salt*

Mix all the ingredients in a small saucepan. Place over very gentle heat, and stir until the sauce thickens. Serve at once.

Sour Cream Salad Dressing 1

For *yolks of 2 hard boiled eggs* allow:

1 *teaspoon sugar*	¼ *pint Sour Cream*
a good pinch of salt	1 *teaspoon chopped parsley,*
a little freshly ground pepper	*fennel or chervil*
1 *tablespoon vinegar*	

Pound together the yolks, sugar and seasoning in a basin. Mix in the vinegar. Gradually stir in the cream, and lastly the herbs.

Sour Cream Salad Dressing 2

Nothing could be simpler than this dressing; it is nice and not as rich as most.

Mix together:

¼ *pint Sour Cream*	½ *teaspoon sugar*
1 *teaspoon vinegar*	*salt and pepper to taste*

Cream Garnish

This cream, which can be passed through a forcing bag, is excellent for decorating sweets and cakes, and also makes a good filling for sponge sandwiches, when suitable flavours can be added.

For *each stiffly whisked egg white* allow:

½ *teaspoon gelatine* soaked in	4 *heaped tablespoons*
1 *teaspoon cold water*	*whipped cream*
3 *teaspoons boiling water*	½–1 *tablespoon caster*
¼ *teaspoon vanilla*	*sugar*

Dissolve the soaked gelatine with the boiling water. Add the vanilla.

Fold into the whisked egg white, first the whipped cream, then the sugar and lastly the gelatine mixture.

Chill well before using.

CREAM CHEESE

Anyone who has an electric liquidizer or a cream machine can, quickly and with very little effort, make their own delicious cream cheeses, with flavours to suit their own taste. When the cheese is mixed with herbs and garlic it can be compared with Boursin, but not in cost.

The Basic Cheese is made with:

>   2 *oz butter*   4 *fluid oz full cream milk*
>   1 *dessertspoon lemon juice, fresh or bottled*

Boil the butter and milk in a small saucepan. Liquidize the mixture, or pump it through a cream machine. Pour it back into the pan and again bring to the boil. Remove from heat and immediately add the lemon juice. Leave for 2 to 3 minutes. Then pour the curdled mixture into a 4½ inch nylon sieve, lined with a piece of white cotton or linen and resting over a pudding basin. Leave for 1 to 1½ hours, no longer, then tip cheese onto a plate.

Now you decide on the flavour.

Savoury Cream Cheeses

When the *Basic Cheese* is made with a salt butter, no extra salt, or very little, will be needed, but pepper, preferably freshly ground, is always necessary. For other flavours choose from the following:

chopped parsley or any herb, fresh or dried, preferably the former	*finely chopped or coarsely ground salted peanuts: these give a delicious flavour*
chopped chives	*chopped capers*
crushed garlic or garlic powder	*chopped olives*
grated onion	*chopped pickles*
	paprika
	a dash of Tabasco or pinch of cayenne

Work the chosen seasoning and additions into the still soft cheese with a pliable knife and pack it into a small container. Leave uncovered until firm. After a few hours, it will have hardened and be ready to serve. The cheese keeps well for several days in or out of the refrigerator.

Do not discard the whey left in the basin; it is excellent in scones (p. 15), gravies and sauces.

Savoury Cream Cheese is used in the following recipes.

Ham and Cheese Rolls, p. 19
Ham and Cheese Fillings, p. 69
Savoury Apple Rings, p. 20
Savoury Bread Slices, p. 20
Savoury Fillings and Spreads, pp. 68–70

Sweet Cream Cheese

This is not served as a cheese. It is a *Basic Cream Cheese*, made with *salt-free butter*, and is used as an ingredient in the following recipes.

Cream Cheese and Kirsch

Served in individual dishes with *fresh or frozen raspberries or fresh pineapple*, this makes a delicious sweet. It is also an excellent filling for pastry cases, especially when these are made with *Almond Cinnamon Pastry* (pp. 38, 40).

To serve 3–4 allow:

THE CREAM CHEESE (BASIC CHEESE, p. 110)

6 *fluid oz milk*   3 *teaspoons lemon juice*
3 *oz salt-free butter*

Allow the cheese to set a little before incorporating:
2 *teaspoons caster sugar*   3 *teaspoons Kirsch*

Continental Cheese Cake

To serve 5–6 allow:

THE CREAM CHEESE (BASIC CHEESE, p. 110)

Make the cream cheese the day before the other filling ingredients are added.

8 *fluid oz milk*   1 *tablespoon lemon juice*
4 *oz salt-free butter*

THE CRUST   Oven Setting 375°F, Mark 5

The crust must be quite cold before it is baked again with the filling, and can well be made the day before.

> 10 *digestive biscuits*   3 *tablespoons moist brown sugar*
> 2 *oz melted butter*   1 *egg yolk*

Crush the biscuits. A good method is to pass them through the fine disc of a Mouli Shredder.

Put the melted butter and sugar in a basin and beat well with a wire or perforated spoon. Add the egg yolk and beat again until well blended. Gradually beat in the crushed biscuits.

Tip the mixture into a loose-bottomed 7 inch cake tin and press it down firmly to cover the bottom and 1–1¼ inches up the sides.

Bake in pre-heated oven for 25–30 minutes. As soon as it comes out of the oven, press the crust into shape again. Leave it in the tin.

THE FILLING   Oven Setting 375°F, Mark 5

> *the made Cream Cheese*   ½ *teaspoon vanilla*
> 2 *egg yolks*   2 *egg whites*
> 2 *tablespoons caster sugar*

Beat the egg yolks and sugar into the cream cheese. Add the vanilla. Whisk the whites until very stiff and fold them carefully into the mixture. Pour this into the crust.

Bake in pre-heated oven for 25 minutes. Reduce heat to 325°F, Mark 3, for another 15 minutes and again to 300°F, Mark 2, for 10 minutes. Turn off the heat, but leave the cheese cake in the oven for about 15 minutes. When using an electric oven, leave the door ajar. The object is to allow the Cheese Cake to cool slowly. Remove from tin when nearly cold by standing it on a jam jar or basin, and pushing down the tin's sides. For parties, decorate Cheese Cake with blobs of whipped cream and glacé cherries.

A larger cheese cake can be made by making the crust given for *Fruit Curd Flan* and increasing all the filling ingredients by 50 per cent.

Fruit Curd Flan

As with *Continental Cheese Cake*, both the cream cheese and crust must be prepared in advance. To serve 8 allow:

THE CREAM CHEESE

This is the same as given for *Continental Cheese Cake.*

THE CRUST   Oven Setting 375°F, Mark 5

14 *digestive biscuits*	4 *tablespoons moist brown sugar*
3 *oz melted butter*	1 *egg yolk*

Follow the instructions given for the crust of the *Continental Cheese Cake,* using an 8 inch loose-bottomed tin.

THE FILLING   Oven Setting 375°F, Mark 5

the made Cream Cheese	1 *oz fresh breadcrumbs*
2 *oz caster sugar*	½ *teaspoon brandy or rum*
1 *egg*	*pinch of nutmeg*
1 *egg yolk*	6 *oz currants or mixed dried fruit*

Gradually add the sugar, egg and egg yolk, crumbs, spirit and nutmeg to the Cream Cheese, beating them in with a wire or perforated spoon. Lastly stir in the fruit.

Pour the mixture into the cooked crust and bake as given for *Continental Cheese Cake.*

Soft Custard

A good soft custard is often appreciated even if there is a constant supply of cream. Cream is sometimes too rich for a sweet, and of course *trifles need custard and cream.*

This custard is delicious, you just can't compare it with one made with custard powder, and it does not take much longer to prepare.

Allow:

2 *tablespoons sugar*	2 *egg yolks*
1 *teaspoon flour*	¾ *pint milk*
a pinch of salt	½ *teaspoon vanilla*

Mix the sugar, flour and salt in the top of a double saucepan, or in a basin.

In another basin, beat the yolks slightly and stir in the milk.

Gradually add the yolk mixture to the sugar mixture, stirring with a wooden spoon. Cook over boiling water, stirring continuously until the custard thickens and coats the spoon. Add the vanilla. Chill.

COOK AHEAD WITH POTATOES

POTATOES become a bugbear when the raw root has to be scrubbed, peeled and cooked before every main meal. However, with the help of a pressure cooker or a steamer,* a cook need never peel a raw potato; yet, whenever potatoes are wanted, these can be quickly prepared and served in many different ways.

This is the method:

Wash as many potatoes as you will need for a week, or your pressure cooker or steamer will hold. They should be as near the same size as possible, if not, halve the larger ones.

Either pressure cook at 15 lbs pressure over $\frac{1}{4}$ pint salted water for 6–20 minutes according to age and size, or steam until tender. Immediately the potatoes are cooked, place them in a wire or perforated plastic container – anything that will not rust and will allow the air to circulate freely – flexible plastic colanders-cum-salad washers are excellent for this purpose and inexpensive. Store in a cool, well ventilated place, not a refrigerator. Now, whenever potatoes are to be served, the skins peel off with ease, speed, without mess, and the potatoes can be prepared and presented according to the following recipes.

Steamed Potatoes

Peel the *cooked potatoes* and reheat them either in a pressure cooker or a steamer.

Pressure cook over $2\frac{1}{2}$ fluid oz salted water for $\frac{1}{4}$ to 1 minute, according to size and number of potatoes. Reduce pressure under a cold tap, and serve.

Steam for 2 to 5 minutes according to size and number of potatoes. Serve as soon as they are really hot.

Steamed Potatoes and Curry Sauce

Place freshly *Steamed Potatoes* in a hot serving dish and pour over them very hot *Curry Sauce* (p. 85).

* Views on pressure cookers and steamers are given on pp. 1–2,

114

New Potatoes

Peel the *cooked new potatoes* and reheat them as given for *Steamed Potatoes,* with the addition of *a sprig of mint.*

Place the hot, reheated potatoes in a hot covered dish containing *a good knob of melted butter.* Add a liberal amount of *chopped parsley or mint.*

Replace cover and shake the dish, so that the potatoes are well coated with butter and the chosen herb.

Small, not-so-young, waxy potatoes can be prepared this way throughout the year and are likely to be acclaimed as 'new potatoes'.

Creamed Potato

Creamed Potatoes are not only excellent with casseroles and many other dishes, but also the base of a number of potato recipes. Therefore it is a good plan, when preparing Creamed Potatoes, to make more than is needed for the one meal. You may have started with cold cooked potatoes, but in a matter of moments you will be serving a piping hot dish.

To serve 2 allow:

about ¾ *lb cooked potatoes*	2–3 *tablespoons milk*
1 *oz butter or margarine*	*salt and pepper to taste*

Peel and mash, grate or shred potatoes. Hot, freshly cooked potatoes are easily mashed with a fork, but cold cooked potatoes are far better either rubbed through a fine grater or passed through a hand or electric shredder.

Heat the fat and milk in a saucepan. When boiling, add the mashed potato, a little at a time, beating continuously with a fork or a perforated spoon. Always allow the mixture to reboil before adding more potato and, if necessary, a little extra milk. Season to taste.

Baked Creamed Potato   Oven Setting 375–400°F, Mark 5–6

This is one of the best and most useful of the Creamed Potato recipes.

Either pack the *Creamed Potato* into a well greased ovenproof pie dish from which it can be served, or mould it into a ring on a shallow ovenproof dish or plate, also suitable for the table.

Bake on top shelf of preheated oven for about 20 minutes, or till brown. The given oven setting is practical when it is only used for Baked

Creamed Potatoes, but if other dishes are cooking at a lower or higher temperature, the Creamed Potato is accommodating and can join these, but will need either more or less time than given.

When baked as a ring, this dish can be filled with *green peas,* other *colourful vegetables,* or with *casseroled meat or poultry.* This makes an attractive party dish.

Fried Potato Balls 1

To serve 3–4 allow:

5–7 *rounded tablespoons Creamed Potato* (p. 115) *according to size of egg*	½ *teaspoon baking powder*
	⅛ *teaspoon salt*
	pinch of paprika
1 *egg*	*a pan of frying oil or fat*

Beat the ingredients until well blended.

Drop the mixture from a teaspoon into the deep hot fat and fry until a golden brown. The balls will need turning.

Drain on absorbent paper and either serve while still hot, or cool, store and reheat as wanted in a hot oven – 425°F, Mark 7.

Baked Potato Balls and Cornflakes

Oven Setting 375°F, Mark 5

This attractive and useful dish can be prepared well in advance, and baked as wanted.

Creamed Potato (p. 115)	2 *tablespoons water*
melted butter	*crushed cornflakes*
or 1 *egg diluted with*	

The potato must be firm enough to handle; if not, a little extra grated potato should be added. Form into balls. Roll these either in melted butter or diluted egg, and then in the cornflakes to coat thickly. Shortly before serving, place in oven until well heated and, if liked, beginning to brown.

Potato Carrot Balls

Oven Setting 400°F, Mark 6

To make 4 balls allow:

4 *tablespoons Creamed Potato* (p. 115)	1 *tablespoon chopped parsley or chives* (optional)
4 *tablespoons finely grated carrot*	*salt and pepper to taste*
	a little melted butter
	brown breadcrumbs

Mix the potato, carrot, herbs and seasoning, and roll into balls.

Coat these in melted butter, then drop one at a time into a small basin of crumbs. Bounce them round until well covered.

Place on a greased baking sheet and bake 20–30 minutes in pre-heated oven, until the carrot is cooked and the balls a pale brown.

Creamed Potato Pancakes

To make 8 pancakes allow:

6 *heaped tablespoons Creamed Potato* (p. 115)
4 *rounded tablespoons self-raising flour*
1 *standard egg*

seasoning to taste
1 *tablespoon chopped parsley* (optional)
butter with 1 *teaspoon oil or lard for frying*

Blend the ingredients. With floured hands, form the mixture into flat cakes.

Fry in hot fat until brown on both sides.

Serve immediately.

Creamed Potato Fritters

Creamed Potato (p. 115)   *Coating Batter* (pp. 17–18)

Form the potato into flat cakes. Leave these for a while on a plate to dry out.

Immediately before the meal, dip each cake in the batter, fry in hot lard and drain on absorbent paper.

Potato Cheese Puffs   Oven Setting 350°F, Mark 4

To make 3 or 4 puffs allow:

1 *egg yolk*
11 *level tablespoons Creamed Potato*
1½ *tablespoons hot milk*
1 *oz finely grated cheese*
⅛ *teaspoon salt*
⅛ *teaspoon paprika*

⅛ *teaspoon celery salt*
a pinch of garlic salt (optional)
1 *teaspoon chopped parsley*
1 *egg white, well whisked*
a little melted butter
grated parmesan

Beat the egg yolk in a basin with a fork or perforated spoon. Add the potato, milk and cheese, and beat again until light and fluffy.

Add the seasoning and parsley.

Fold in the stiff egg white.

Place the mixture in 3 or 4 mounds on a greased baking tin. Brush these with melted butter and sprinkle with parmesan.

Bake in pre-heated oven for 20 minutes.

Potato and Cheese Volcanoes

These make an excellent luncheon or supper dish.

For each serving allow:

about 3 heaped tablespoons Creamed   *a little melted butter*
   Potato (p. 115), not too moist   *brown breadcrumbs*
about 1½ heaped tablespoons
   Cheese Foundation (p. 7)

Place each serving of potato on to individual oven plates and form into mounds with holes in the centres. Smooth sides with a knife, sloping them towards the top.

Fill the holes with the Cheese Foundation, allowing this to come higher than the potato.

Brush potato with butter and sprinkle with crumbs.

The volcanoes can be prepared to this stage well in advance.

Shortly before serving, either heat and brown them under the grill, or bake them in the oven, 425°F, Mark 7, until brown.

This dish can be prepared as one large volcano, and in that case it must be baked.

Potato Fritters

Cold cooked potatoes   *Coating Batter* (pp. 17–18)

Peel potatoes and cut into thick slices.

Dip in Coating Batter, fry and drain on absorbent paper.

Battered Potato Slices

Cold cooked potatoes   *Coating Batter* (pp. 17–18)

As only very little Coating Batter is needed, this dish should be made with *Surplus Coating Batter* (p. 18).

Put this into a small basin and beat well with a fork.

Slice the peeled potatoes, toss them into the batter and stir gently so that they are coated but not broken. Place slices separately into a pan of hot lard and fry on both sides. Drain on absorbent paper.

Roast Potatoes   Oven Setting 425–50°F, Mark 7–8

Pressure cooked or steamed potatoes roast splendidly. They are also quicker to prepare than raw potatoes and need less fat.

Peel potatoes, if large, cut them in half, then put them in a baking tin with *good dripping or lard.*

Place baking tin on top shelf of pre-heated oven. After about 10 minutes remove tin from oven, turn the potatoes so that they have a complete coating of fat. Then pour off all the fat remaining in the tin. Return the potatoes to the oven until they are nice and brown. They will need turning now and then. The whole process should take about 30 minutes.

Mock Roast Potatoes

When *cooked potatoes* are fried and browned in *a little good lard*, they will easily pass as roast potatoes and take far less time to prepare.

Crumbed Potatoes   Oven Setting 400°F, Mark 6

To serve 2 allow:

about ¾ lb cold cooked potatoes   *3–4 tablespoons fine fresh bread-*
2 oz butter or margarine   *crumbs*
                                        salt and pepper to taste

Peel and slice potatoes and put them in a small baking tin with the fat.

Bake in pre-heated oven for about 5 minutes, then add the crumbs and seasoning. Mix well and return to the oven for a further 10–15 minutes, until the potatoes and crumbs are crisp and brown.

Scalloped Potatoes and Bacon   Oven Setting as convenient

To serve 4 allow:

1–1½ lbs cooked potatoes   *salt and pepper to taste*
2 bacon rashers, chopped   *a little nutmeg* (optional)
2 tablespoons Basic Cream Sauce   *brown breadcrumbs*
6 tablespoons milk   *a little butter*
2 tablespoons chopped parsley

Peel and slice the potatoes and place them and the bacon in a greased oven dish.

Heat the Cream Sauce and milk in a small pan and stir in the parsley and seasoning. Pour sauce over the potatoes and bacon. Mix well and top with breadcrumbs dotted with dabs of butter.

Bake in pre-heated oven until brown.

Scalloped Potatoes and Onions   Oven Setting 350°F, Mark 4

To serve 4 allow:

1–1½ lbs cooked potatoes	salt and pepper
1 large onion	3–4 oz butter
a little flour	¼ pint milk

Peel and slice the potatoes and onion.

Grease a baking dish. Fill it with alternate layers of potato and onion. Sprinkle each layer with a little flour and seasoning and dot with butter. Pour over the milk.

Bake in a pre-heated oven for about 45 minutes, or until the top layer of potatoes is crisp and brown.

Pilgrim Potatoes   Oven Setting 350°F, Mark 4

This is a dish which has been popular in the Trappist Monasteries for generations.

To serve 5 allow:

4 tablespoons flour	2 onions, sliced
1 egg	2½–3 lbs cooked potatoes, peeled
½ pint milk	and sliced
a little chopped parsley	breadcrumbs
salt and pepper	a little butter

Beat together in a basin the flour, egg, milk and chopped parsley. Add the sliced potatoes and onions and seasoning. Mix well and transfer to greased oven dish. Cover with breadcrumbs and dot with butter.

Bake in pre-heated oven until well browned.

Chips

Cooked potatoes, provided they are not floury, or over-cooked, make really excellent chips. These, like orthodox chips made from raw potatoes, are best when fried in deep fat, preferably oil, but they cook in a fraction of the time.

Crispy Potatoes   Oven Setting 400°F, Mark 6

fairly waxy cooked potatoes	salt and pepper to taste
lard or dripping	

Pass potatoes through the medium disc of a hand or electric shredder.

Stack them lightly and not too deeply in a baking tin with seasoning and a little fat.

Bake in pre-heated oven for about 40 minutes, or until they are crisp and brown, turning the potatoes now and then.

If necessary during the baking process, add more fat or pour off any surplus.

Sautéed Potatoes

To serve 2 allow:

about ¾ lb cold cooked potatoes	*salt to taste*
1 *or more tablespoons fat*	*a little paprika* (optional)

Peel and slice the potatoes. Melt fat in a frying pan, and when hot add the potato and seasoning. Sauté, turning frequently, until the potatoes are a light brown.

Potatoes Sautés à la Lyonnaise

To serve 2 allow:

about ¾ lb cold cooked potatoes	*about 3 oz onion and a little extra*
a good ½ oz butter, with	*butter*
1 *teaspoon olive oil, or ¾ oz lard*	*salt and pepper to taste*
	a little chopped parsley

Peel the potatoes and cut them into thin round slices.

Heat in a frying pan, either the butter and oil, or the lard, and cook the potatoes to a pale brown.

Slice the onion thinly and evenly. Fry in a small pan in a little hot butter until a light golden colour, but not brown.

Add the cooked onion to the cooked potato and sprinkle with salt, pepper and parsley.

Bubble and Squeak

To serve 2 allow:

about ½ lb cooked potatoes	*cold cooked green vegetables, any kind*
2 *tablespoons good dripping*	*salt and pepper to taste*
1 *small onion, sliced*	*a little vinegar* (optional)

Peel potatoes and mash roughly with a fork.

Heat fat in a frying pan and cook onion until transparent.

Add the potatoes, greens and seasoning and mash together. Lower the heat and cover pan with a lid or plate.

C.A.—E

Cook for about 20 minutes, turning the mixture several times with a slice, so that it will brown as much as possible without burning.

Add the vinegar towards the end of the cooking.

Fried Potato Balls 2

To serve 2 allow:

about 10 oz cooked potatoes	1 egg white
1 egg yolk	brown breadcrumbs
salt to taste	a pan of frying oil or fat
a little nutmeg (optional)	

Peel potatoes and mash, finely grate or shred. Add egg yolk and seasoning.

Form mixture into small balls. Roll these in egg white and crumbs. Fry in deep fat.

Hamburg Potato Balls

To serve 2–3 allow:

about ½ lb cooked potatoes	salt and pepper to taste
½ oz butter or margarine	2 egg whites lightly whisked
2 egg yolks	a pan of oil or fat for deep frying
a jug of very hot water	

Peel the potatoes, and mash with a fork, grate, or pass through the fine disc of a hand or electric shredder.

Melt the fat in a saucepan, add the potato and egg yolks. Stir over gentle heat for a few minutes. Remove from heat and fold in the egg whites.

Using two teaspoons, drop the mixture into the hot oil by scooping it out of one spoon with the help of the other. Dip the spoons in the hot water before each ball is formed. Fry these a light brown and drain on absorbent paper.

Hash-browned Potatoes

To serve 2 allow:

about ¾ lb cold cooked potatoes	4 fluid oz creamy milk, single
1 tablespoon flour	cream or evaporated milk
½ teaspoon salt	1 oz butter or 2 tablespoons oil

Peel and roughly chop the potatoes. Add, and mix in the flour and salt. Stir in the milk without breaking the potatoes.

Heat fat in an 8 inch frying pan, and drop into it large spoonfuls of the potato mixture. Brown these well on both sides.

Baked Potato Cakes   Oven setting 450°F, Mark 8

These are good for parties, as they can be prepared well in advance, even the day before, to be baked shortly before serving.

To make about 20 cakes allow:

about 1½ lbs cooked potato   *pepper to taste*
2 oz butter   *2 egg yolks*
¼ pint milk   *4 tablespoons self-raising flour*
½ teaspoon salt   *2 egg whites, stiffly whisked*

Peel, mash, finely grate or shred the potatoes.
Heat the butter, milk and seasoning in a saucepan.
Beat in the potato, egg yolks and flour and fold in the egg whites.
Spoon the mixture into small, well-oiled or buttered foil baking cases.
Bake in pre-heated oven for about 15 minutes or until the cakes are a pale brown. To eject them, invert cakes on a hot dish and gently press the bottoms of the foil cases.

Potatoes à l'Indienne

cooked potatoes   Sauce Indienne (pp. 77–8)

Peel and slice the potatoes, and either put them in a flame-proof casserole, a saucepan or an oven dish. Mix in plenty of the sauce.

Heat through, either over gentle heat, stirring now and then, or covered, in the oven.

Piquant Potatoes

To serve 2 allow:

about ¾ lb cooked potatoes   *hot water*
2–3 rashers streaky bacon,   *vinegar, salt and sugar to taste*
* cut up*
1½ teaspoons flour

Peel and cut potatoes into thick slices.
Slowly cook the bacon in a covered pan over gentle heat, and when it has exuded enough fat, stir in the flour. Cook for about a minute, then

slowly add enough water to make a fairly thick sauce. Cook until this thickens, then flavour with vinegar, salt and sugar.

Add potatoes, and simmer over very low heat until they are warmed through, or the mixture can be transferred to a casserole and heated in the oven.

Potato au Gratin

To serve 2 allow:

about ¾ lb cooked potatoes	brown breadcrumbs
4–5 tablespoons Cheese Sauce 1 or 2	grated cheese
(pp. 7, 85)	

Peel and slice the potatoes and place them in a greased oven dish.

Heat the Cheese Sauce in a pan and pour it over the potato. Mix them together and cover with crumbs and grated cheese.

Heat through and brown, either in the oven or under the grill.

Potato au Gratin Variations

Other foods can be added to the potato before the Cheese Sauce is added: these not only provide a change, but a more substantial dish.

For example:

sliced hard boiled eggs	slices of cooked ham
sliced Frankfurters or cooked sausages	minced meat left overs

Potato and Cheese Moulds   Oven Setting 375°F, Mark 5

To serve 4–5 allow:

about ¾ lb cooked potatoes	5 eggs
4 oz grated cheese	salt and pepper to taste
3 tablespoons Sour Cream (pp. 105–6)	

Peel and grate the potatoes, mix them with the cheese and cream.

Beat in the eggs. A little more cream can be added, if too firm. Season.

Put the mixture in oiled or buttered Alcan foil cases, dishes or little basins and bake in pre-heated oven for about 30 minutes or until cooked and a pale brown.

To eject moulds, invert them on to a hot dish and gently press the foil bottoms.

Shepherd Potato   Oven Setting 375°F, Mark 5

To serve 4 allow:

1 *lb cooked potatoes*   *salt and pepper to taste*
1 *onion, finely chopped*   1 *beaten egg*
1 *oz butter or margarine*   1 *oz grated cheese*
1 *tablespoon chopped parsley*

Peel, then mash the potatoes in a mixing bowl.

Melt the butter or margarine in a frying pan and gently fry the onion until soft but not discoloured. Add this to the potato, together with the parsley, seasoning and beaten egg and mix well.

Transfer the mixture to a greased oven dish, cover the top with the grated cheese, and bake in pre-heated oven until crisp and brown.

Potato and Cheese Pie   Oven Setting 350°F, Mark 4

To serve 4 allow:

1 *lb cooked potatoes*   *salt and pepper to taste*
2 *eggs*   *a little butter*
¾ *pint milk*   4 *oz grated cheese*

Peel and slice the potatoes. Beat the eggs thoroughly. Add the milk and seasoning and beat again.

Butter an oven dish and cover the bottom with a layer of sliced potato. Sprinkle with about ⅓ of the cheese and about ⅓ of the egg and milk. Repeat this twice more.

Bake in pre-heated oven for about 30 minutes.

Potatoes à la Provencale

To serve 4–5 allow:

1½ *lbs cooked potatoes*   ¼ *pint milk*
3 *oz grated Gruyère,*   *salt and pepper*
    Emmenthal or Jarlsberg   *chopped parsley*
    cheese
1–2 *oz butter*

Peel the potatoes, and finely grate or shred.

Mix the cheese and butter to a paste. Add the milk and chopped parsley.

Pour this mixture into a hot frying pan, stir in the potato and season to taste. Fry till a pale brown. Serve.

Potato and Gruyère Triangles

1 *lb cooked potatoes*	*a little garlic salt* (optional)
salt and pepper	*browned breadcrumbs*
6 *portions of Gruyère cheese*	*fat for frying*
beaten egg	

Peel potatoes, and mash, or finely grate or shred. Season well and divide into 6 portions. Press each one flat, place a triangle of cheese in the centre and mould the potato round it, taking care that the cheese is entirely covered. Shape into neat triangles.

Add a little garlic salt to the beaten egg if liked. Dip each triangle into the egg, cover with breadcrumbs and fry in hot fat until crisp and golden brown.

Drain on absorbent paper and serve.

Cheese and Potato Balls

To serve 4–5 allow:

about 1½ *lbs cooked potatoes*	1 *egg and* 1 *egg yolk*
½ *oz butter or margarine*	*fresh breadcrumbs* (*fine*)
2 *oz grated cheese*	*a pan of hot frying oil*
pepper and salt to taste	

Peel potatoes and mash, or finely grate or shred them.

Put them in a saucepan with the fat, cheese, seasoning and the egg yolk. Stir with a fork or perforated spoon over gentle heat until the fat and cheese have melted and the egg yolk has cooked. Turn mixture on to a plate and leave until cold.

Divide into equal portions and form into balls. Beat the egg in a small basin and put the crumbs in another. Drop the balls one at a time first into the egg and then into the crumbs.

Deep fry these until a golden brown. Drain on absorbent paper.

Serve very hot, if liked with *fried parsley*.

Fried Potato Cakes and Cheese

To serve 2–3 allow:

2 *thick slices stale bread*	1 *tablespoon chopped chives*
a little milk	*or grated onion* (optional)
about ½ *lb cooked potato*	*salt and pepper to taste*
2 *eggs*	*butter and oil for frying*
1 *dessertspoon flour*	*grated cheese*

Soak the bread in milk, strain and put in a basin.

Peel and grate or shred the potato and add to the bread, together with the eggs, flour, chives and seasoning. Mix well and form into flat roundcakes.

Fry these on both sides in hot butter to which a teaspoon of olive oil has been added. Drain on absorbent paper.

Just before serving, sprinkle well with grated cheese and brown under the grill.

Potato and Pepper au Gratin   Oven Setting 375°F, Mark 5

To serve 6 allow:

about 1½ lbs cold cooked potatoes	salt to taste
1 green pepper, seeded and chopped	½ teaspoon paprika
1 onion, chopped	a few grains cayenne
1 tablespoon flour	8 fluid oz full cream milk
3 oz grated cheese	brown bread crumbs
	a little butter

Peel and dice the potatoes into a bowl. Mix in the pepper, onion, flour, cheese and seasoning.

Transfer to a greased oven dish and pour the milk over the mixture. Cover with crumbs and dot with butter.

Bake on top shelf of pre-heated oven for about 35 minutes.

Russian Potatoes   Oven Setting 375°F, Mark 5

To serve 2 allow:

¾ lbs cooked potatoes	2 tablespoons grated cheese
¼ oz butter	1 egg
1 small onion, chopped	¼ pint Sour Cream (pp. 105–6)
2 tablespoons fresh breadcrumbs (fine)	salt and pepper to taste

Peel and slice the potatoes into an oven dish.

Melt the butter in a small pan and fry the onion to a golden brown. Mix these, the crumbs and cheese with the potato.

Beat the egg into the Sour Cream, add the seasoning and pour over the potato mixture.

Bake in pre-heated oven for about 20 minutes, or until brown.

Sweet Corn Potatoes

To serve 4 allow:

about 1 *lb cooked potatoes*
1 *small onion (grated)*
2 *tablespoons fat or salad oil*
an 11 *oz tin sweet corn (whole kernels)*

1 *teaspoon chopped parsley*
¼ *teaspoon salt*
a little pepper

Peel and dice the potatoes.

Fry the onion in the fat or salad oil in a saucepan until clear. Stir in the potatoes and other ingredients and heat through, stirring occasionally. Serve very hot.

Potato and Sausage Pie   Oven Setting 425°F, Mark 7

To serve 2 allow:

about ¾ *lb cooked potatoes*
4–6 *sausages*
1 *egg*

½ *teaspoon made mustard (optional)*
salt and pepper to taste

Peel, and slice the potatoes into a baking tin and lay the sausages on top. Cook in pre-heated oven until the sausages are brown on top. Turn them and return to oven to brown the other sides.

Remove the sausages from the baking tin and fit them snugly into an oven dish.

Mash together the potato and fat from the sausages with a fork. Add the egg and seasoning and beat in. When completely blended, spread the mixture over the sausages and put back in the oven until nice and brown.

Hungarian Egg and Potato Pie   Oven Setting 375°F, Mark 5

This is a delicious and substantial dish for any meal.

To serve 2 allow:

about ¾ *lb cooked potatoes*
2 *slices of cooked ham, cut*
   into strips
½ *pint Sour Cream (pp. 105–6)*
2 *hard boiled eggs, sliced*

1 *small cooked cauliflower,*
   divided into flowerettes
brown breadcrumbs
a little melted butter

Peel and slice the potatoes and put half of them on the bottom of a well greased oven dish. Lay the ham on top and cover with some of the sour cream. Add a layer of egg, again covered with cream, and then the cauliflower with more cream. The rest of the potato constitutes the final layer, and this is covered with the remaining cream.

Lastly sprinkle with crumbs and pour over a little melted butter.

Bake 20–25 minutes or till brown in the pre-heated oven.

Potato and Ham Soufflé   Oven Setting 375°F, Mark 5

To serve 2–3 allow:

about ¾ lb cooked potatoes	1 teaspoon made mustard
½ oz butter or margarine	2 egg yolks
4 tablespoons milk or cream	pepper and salt to taste
5–8 tablespoons minced ham	2 whisked egg whites

Peel and mash, grate or shred the potatoes.

Melt the fat in a saucepan. Remove from heat and add the liquid. Stir in the potato. Beat well and add the ham, mustard, egg yolks and seasoning.

When all the ingredients are blended, fold in the well whisked egg white.

Pour mixture into a greased soufflé or oven dish.

Bake in pre-heated oven for 30 minutes. Serve hot.

Ham Potatoes   Oven Setting 375°F, Mark 5

This is a good way of finishing the remains of ham or bacon joints and the proportional quantities of potato and ham are a matter of choice and expediency.

Use:

slices of cooked potato	one of the Savoury Cream Sauces
minced cooked ham or bacon	(pp. 85–6)
	a little grated cheese

Mix the potato and ham with plenty of the chosen sauce and place in a greased oven dish. Sprinkle the top with cheese and bake in pre-heated oven for about 30 minutes.

Baked Herring Potatoes   Oven Setting 375°F, Mark 5

This is a tasty luncheon or supper dish from Germany.

To serve 2–3 allow:

1 lb cooked potatoes	1 egg yolk
a few pickled gherkins	6 fluid oz Sour Cream (pp. 105–6)
(optional)	1 oz butter
2 pickled herrings	½ oz grated parmesan

Peel and slice the potatoes, and, when using gherkins, slice and mix these with the potatoes.

Cut the herrings into dice.

Place alternate layers of potato and herring in a buttered oven dish, beginning and ending with potato.

Beat the yolk into the Sour Cream and pour it over the potato.

Dot with small pieces of butter and sprinkle with cheese.

Bake about 30 minutes in pre-heated oven.

Potato and Shrimp Savouries   Oven Setting 350°F, Mark 4

This makes a good party luncheon dish.

To serve 6–8 allow:

2 *lbs cooked potatoes*	*brown breadcrumbs*
4 *oz cheese*	$\frac{3}{4}$ *oz flour*
4 *oz butter or margarine*	$7\frac{1}{2}$ *fluid oz milk*
2 *egg yolks*	$\frac{3}{4}$ *pint of shrimps, fresh, tinned or*
salt and pepper to taste	*frozen*

Garnish: *a sprig of parsley or watercress*

Peel the potatoes, mash or finely grate or shred them into a saucepan. Add 2 oz of the cheese and 1 oz of the fat. Stir over gentle heat until the cheese has melted. Remove from heat.

Beat up the yolks and stir them and the seasoning into the potato. Turn mixture on to a lightly floured surface, divide into 6 or 8 equal portions and mould each into the shape of a small basin. Smooth the outside and top edges with a knife.

Melt about 2 oz of the butter, brush it over the moulds, coat with the breadcrumbs and place them on a greased baking sheet.

Bake in pre-heated oven, while the shrimp filling is prepared as follows:

Melt the remaining butter in a small pan, stir in the flour, and when well mixed gradually add the milk. Stir until the sauce boils, then simmer for a few minutes. Add the shrimps and remaining cheese. Continue stirring until the cheese has melted. Season.

Fill the hot moulds with this sauce. Place on a heated serving dish or individual plates and keep hot until required.

Before serving, garnish with sprigs of parsley or watercress.

Fried Potato Pies

To make 4 pies allow:

THE CRUST

1 *lb cooked potatoes*	½ *teaspoon freshly ground*
2 *oz self-raising flour*	*pepper*
1 *oz melted butter or margarine*	½ *teaspoon salt*

THE FILLING

Any of the *Fillings* given for *Small Pies* (pp. 63, 64, 68, 69).

Peel potatoes and mash, grate or shred them into a mixing bowl. Add the flour, fat and seasoning and mix into a firm dough. If necessary, add a little extra flour.

Divide dough into eight portions. Place these on a floured surface and roll into rounds of equal size. Put about 1½ tablespoons of the chosen filling in the centre of four of the rounds. (*Curry Filling*, pp. 64–5, is very good in these pies.) Damp the dough surrounding the fillings with a little milk and cover with the remaining rounds. Press the edges together, turn the two edges towards the centre of the pies and press again. Dust with a little flour, and deep fry in *a good frying oil* until a golden brown. Drain on absorbent paper.

Serve very hot, if liked, with *a Savoury Sauce*.

COOK AHEAD WITH APPLES

APPLE PURÉE is needed in many recipes. This does not take long to make, but means another job before the dish itself can be prepared. To have a constant supply of apple purée throughout the year is therefore a great asset, especially when apples are expensive, and money as well as time is saved. It is when apples are plentiful and windfalls (which are quite adequate) can be had for the asking or collecting, that the purée should be made in bulk and either bottled by any of the recognized fruit bottling methods (see p. 133), or stored in containers in a deep freeze.

How to Make Apple Purée

There are two ways of making this purée, one in a pressure-cooker and the other in a large saucepan. The first is certainly much quicker and more carefree.

In both methods, the apples are neither peeled nor cored, just washed, dried, and any bad pieces cut out.

Remember when following apple recipes that the purée is already sweetened and less or no extra sugar will be needed. It is also useful to know that:

about ¾ pint of purée = 1 lb apples

Apple Purée 1

Made in a pressure-cooker

Cut the apples into rough pieces, about the size of plums. Place in a pressure-cooker *over 2½ fluid oz water*. Cook at 15 lbs pressure for 1 to 3 minutes according to quantity and type of apples. Reduce pressure.

Pass the fruit through the medium disc of a Moulin Legumes.

Measure the purée and pour it back into the cooker, adding:

3 to 6 oz sugar to each pint of apple

Stir over heat and boil for about 3 minutes, stirring continuously.

Pour either into hot jars and sterilize by chosen method, or into containers for storing in a deep freeze.

Apple Purée 2

Made in a large saucepan.

Weigh the apples, and cut them into rough pieces, about the size of damsons. Place in a large saucepan.

Add: $\frac{1}{4}$ *pint water for each* 1 *lb apples.*

Cover pan and place over very gentle heat, stirring frequently until the simmering apples begin to mush.

Raise heat and stir continuously allowing the apples to boil rapidly without burning until most of the water has evaporated and the mixture is spitting instead of bubbling.

Pass the fruit through the medium disc of a Moulin Legumes and continue as given for *Apple Purée* 1.

Two good methods for bottling *Apple Purée* are:

1. The Oven Method   Oven Setting 275°F, Mark 1

Pour the purée into the jars to within about 1 inch of the top.

Put on rubber rings and glass tops or sealing discs.

Adjust metal screw tops by screwing as tightly as possible and then loosening them by half a turn.

Place jars in central position of pre-heated oven, standing on asbestos mats or cardboard. Space must be allowed between the jars. Cook 45 minutes.

Remove jars and place on a wooden or formica surface, away from draught. Tighten screw tops. After a few hours tighten tops again.

Leave jars for 24 hours. Test the seals and store in a cool dry place.

2. The Pressure Cooker Method

All pressure cookers are sold with their own books of instructions. Follow the directions given for the bottling of fruit purée.

Apple Purée Recipes

Apple Sauce

Heated *Apple Purée* supplies an ever-ready Apple Sauce. This, however, can be improved by the addition of:

a little butter or margarine

Apple Compôte

This enriched *Apple Purée* is delicious served with cream, custard, milk puddings or as fillings for *Pastry Cases* (pp. 38–42) or *Pancakes* (pp. 24–5).

For each 3 tablespoons of Apple Purée allow:

¼ *oz butter*	⅛ *teaspoon cinnamon or*
½–1 *tablespoon currants*	*powdered cloves* (optional)
a little extra sugar, if needed	

Place the purée, butter, sugar and spice in a saucepan and stir over gentle heat. Allow to simmer for about 2 minutes, stirring continuously. Serve hot or cold.

Apple Meringue   Oven Setting 275°F, Mark 1

To serve 4 allow:

1 *pint Apple Purée*	1 *lemon*
additional sugar, if needed	2 *eggs*
	4 *oz caster sugar*

Put in a basin the sweetened apple, the finely grated lemon rind, the lemon juice and egg yolks. Beat well and pour the mixture into a greased oven dish.

Whisk the egg whites until very stiff and gradually fold in the caster sugar. Pile the meringue on top of the apple.

Bake for 50 minutes in pre-heated oven.

Serve hot, with custard, or cold, with whipped cream or custard.

Apple Orange Amber   Oven Setting 400°F, Mark 6

To serve 3–4 allow:

THE CRUMB MIXTURE

1½ *oz melted butter*	¼ *pint fresh breadcrumbs*
3 *tablespoons Demerara sugar*	*rind of* 1 *orange, finely grated*

THE APPLE MIXTURE

10 *tablespoons Apple Purée*	*the orange, cut into pieces after*
additional sugar, if needed	*removing as much skin and pith*
	as possible

TOPPING

    2 *tablespoons brown breadcrumbs*   ¼ *oz butter*
    1 *tablespoon Demerara sugar*

Blend the Crumb Mixture ingredients. Mix the orange pieces with the sweetened apple.

Place a third of the crumb mixture on the bottom of a greased oven dish, and cover with half the apple and orange. Repeat these layers and spread over the remaining crumb mixture.

Top with the brown crumbs mixed with the sugar and dot with small pieces of butter.

Bake 20 minutes in pre-heated oven.

Serve hot with: custard, a *Hard Sauce* (p. 82), *Orange Syrup* (p. 83), or *Orange Cream Sauce* (p. 88), or cold with: cream or custard.

This sweet is especially good when cold.

Apple Snow and Custard

To serve 4 allow:

THE SNOW

    1 *dessertspoon powdered gelatine*   6 *tablespoons Apple Purée,*
    5 *teaspoons lemon juice, fresh*   *chilled*
       or bottled   *additional sugar, if needed*
    2½ *tablespoons boiling water*   2 *egg whites*

THE CUSTARD

  see *Soft Custard*, p. 113.

TO DECORATE

      glacé cherries   *angelica*   *whipped cream* (optional)

Put the gelatine in a cup with the lemon juice.

When soaked, add the boiling water, stir well until dissolved, pour this into the sweetened apple and stir well.

Whisk the egg whites until stiff, and fold them into the apple mixture.

Spoon the snow into individual sundae glasses or into a serving bowl.

Make the *Soft Custard* using the surplus egg yolks, and when cold, pour it over the apple.

Decorate.

Danish Apple Cake

This delicious sweet is very quick to prepare and requires no cooking, provided the crumbs and apple are in stock.

Use a loose-bottomed cake tin or a soufflé dish.

FOR THE CAKE

    Sweet Fried Crumbs (p. 201)   *Apple Purée or Apple Compôte*

DECORATIONS

    blobs of raspberry jam and   *walnuts or chopped almonds*
    whipped cream

Place in the container alternate layers of Sweet Fried Crumbs and either Apple Purée or Apple Compôte, starting and finishing with a layer of crumbs.

Press firmly and allow to set before unmoulding and decorating.

Apple Almond Pudding   Oven Setting 375°F, Mark 5

To serve 4 allow:

    ¾ pint Apple Purée   *4 oz caster sugar*
    2 oz fresh breadcrumbs   *1 egg*
    additional sugar, if needed   *1½ oz ground almonds*
    3 oz butter or margarine, warmed   *a few chopped blanched almonds*

Blend the sweetened purée and breadcrumbs, and place in a greased oven dish.

Cream the fat and sugar, beat in the egg, and stir in the ground almonds.

Cover the apples with this mixture. Sprinkle with chopped almonds.

Bake 40 minutes in pre-heated oven.

Serve cold.

Apple Charlotte   Oven Setting 375°F, Mark 5

This is a simple but good sweet:

    thin slices of bread   *additional sugar, if needed*
    melted butter   *fresh or preserved grated lemon*
    brown sugar   *or orange rind* (p. 167)
    Apple Purée   *1 or 2 eggs*

Cut sufficient bread to line an oven dish and to cover the pudding. The slices should overlap each other.

Dip the bread first in butter, then in brown sugar.

Line the buttered dish.

Add the lemon or orange rind to the sweetened purée and beat in the egg.

Pour the mixture into the lined dish and cover with the remaining butter- and sugar-coated bread slices.

Bake in pre-heated oven for about 30 minutes.

Turn pudding out on to a hot dish and serve with: custard, a *Hard Sauce* (p. 82), *Lemon or Orange Syrup* (p. 83) *or Orange Cream Sauce* (p. 88).

Apple Scone Pudding   Oven Setting 375°F, Mark 5

To serve 4–5 allow:

1 *pint Apple Purée*	8 *oz self-raising flour*
additional sugar, if needed	1½ *oz sugar*
2 *oz butter or margarine*	*milk to mix*

Put the sweetened purée into a pie dish and place in the oven.

Rub the fat into the flour. Add the sugar and sufficient milk to make a soft dough.

Place this on a floured surface, and pat into shape – it should just fit inside the top of the dish.

As soon as the apple is bubbling, place the scone cover on top of it, and return to the oven.

When cooked, sprinkle with sugar. Serve hot with custard or a *Hard Sauce* (p. 82).

Apple Purée is also used in the following recipes:

Sausage Pancakes, p. 26
Apple Crumb Flan, p. 51
Apple Curd Flan, p. 52
Apple Shortcake, p. 174
Cape Town Apple Tart, p. 175
Copenhagen Fruit Pie, pp. 175–6
Layer Pudding, p. 177
Swedish Apple Pudding, p. 175
Swiss Apple Tart, p. 51
Fillings (pp. 72–3) for **Flans, Tartlet Cases, Turnovers and Pancakes**
Apple Sauce Cake, p. 155

CAKE FOUNDATION

INNUMERABLE recipes begin 'Cream the butter and sugar until light and fluffy, then add the well beaten egg'. When time presses this task may well be a deterrent, and no cakes, biscuits or sponge puddings will be made.

With an adequate supply of Cake Foundation sitting in the larder, this situation need never arise. The Foundation is easy and quick to make and will keep for up to three weeks, or even longer provided fresh eggs are used. Once made, all that is needed is the addition of further ingredients to turn the Foundation into sponges, scones, biscuits, cakes – the plainest to the richest wedding cake – savouries and a variety of puddings.

You can use a spoonful or a pound or so, and provide cakes – either a few tiny ones for a doll's party or a batch for a charity fête.

A cake will take no longer to prepare with this Foundation than it does with a commercially packeted Cake Mix. It will most certainly be cheaper – all the ingredients are known to you – and the one Foundation will give a far greater variety than numerous packets.

Cake Foundation can be used for any recipe that includes no less than 4 *oz each of shortening and sugar, and one egg*. This is the content of 10 *oz Cake Foundation*. Thus you can arrive at the same recipe by adding to 10 oz Foundation. all the ingredients over and above the 4 oz shortening, 4 oz sugar and one egg. For example, here is a comparison between the recipe for an orthodox Victoria Sandwich and the same recipe made with Cake Foundation.

Orthodox Sandwich	Cake Foundation Sandwich
4 *oz butter or margarine*	10 *oz Cake Foundation*
4 *oz caster sugar*	1 *egg*
2 *eggs*	4 *oz self-raising flour*
4 *oz self-raising flour*	1 *tablespoon warm water*
1 *tablespoon warm water*	

Recipes with no additional shortening, sugar or egg can be halved by using 5 oz Cake Foundation and adding half of all the remaining ingredients. This is useful when the recipe as it stands will produce more than is needed.

How to make Cake Foundation

Ingredients:

> 1 *lb butter or margarine*
> 1 *lb caster sugar*
> 4 *eggs, weighing about 8 oz*

PROCEDURE BY HAND

When making Cake Foundation by hand, it may be found easier and quicker to divide all the ingredients into two and mix these in two mixing bowls – one of these should be large enough to store the whole amount of prepared Foundation.

1. Place $\frac{1}{2}$ lb of butter or margarine in each mixing bowl – if hard, the fat should be warmed for a few minutes in the oven until soft but not oily.

2. Beat the softened fat with a wire or perforated spoon.

3. Add $\frac{1}{2}$ lb sugar to each $\frac{1}{2}$ lb of fat, beating all the time until the mixture is light and creamy.

4. Break 2 of the eggs into a basin. Beat them with a fork, not a rotary whisk, until the whites and yolks are completely blended.

5. Add this to one of the fat and sugar mixtures, a little at a time, until completely blended.

6. and 7. Repeat 4 and 5 with the remaining eggs, fat and sugar.

8. Transfer the mixture from the one mixing bowl to the bowl in which the whole amount of Cake Foundation is to be stored and then give the lot a final beating.

For storage see p. 140.

PROCEDURE WITH A HAND ELECTRIC MIXER

The mixture being somewhat bulky for a light machine, it may be found easier to blend the ingredients in two mixing bowls.

1. Place $\frac{1}{2}$ lb butter or margarine in each mixing bowl. If hard, warm for a few minutes in the oven until soft but not oily.

2. Beat the softened fat at high speed for about half a minute.

3. Add $\frac{1}{2}$ lb sugar to each $\frac{1}{2}$ lb fat. Beat until the mixture is light and creamy.

4. Add an egg to the mixtures in both bowls. Beat at low speed, just long enough to incorporate the eggs.

5. Repeat stage 4.

6. Transfer the mixture from the one basin to the other in which the whole amount of Cake Foundation is to be stored.

For storage see below.

PROCEDURE WITH A STANDARD ELECTRIC MIXER

1. Place the butter or margarine in the mixing bowl. If hard, warm for a few minutes in the oven until soft but not oily.

2. Beat the softened fat at high speed for about half a minute.

3. Add the sugar. Beat until the mixture is light and creamy.

4. Break the eggs into the mixture one at a time, beating each at low speed, just long enough to incorporate it, before adding the next one.

5. Transfer the mixture to its storing bowl.

STORAGE OF CAKE FOUNDATION

Cake Foundation should not be stored in a refrigerator, except in very hot climates, but in a cool place, covered against flies and dust.

Deep-freeze owners may find it convenient to weigh out their freshly made Cake Foundation into 10 oz portions and to put each portion into a container to be kept in the deep-freeze until required.

How to use Cake Foundation

To save time and unnecessary washing up, weigh the needed quantity of Foundation in your mixing bowl, naturally adding the weight of the empty bowl to the required weight of Cake Foundation. A real mixing bowl is imperative – do not use a basin.

How, and in which order, to incorporate the ingredients which, according to the recipe, are added to Cake Foundation

1. FATS

When a recipe requires extra butter or margarine, put this in the mixing bowl before weighing the Foundation. As this is rarely soft enough to cream easily, it can be warmed slightly in the oven, but not allowed to become oily.

2. CAKE FOUNDATION

When additional fat is in the bowl, weigh the required Foundation on top of it, discounting the combined weight of the fat and the bowl. The recently warmed bowl and fat will also soften the Foundation and they can easily be beaten and blended.

When the recipe requires no additional fat and the Foundation is cold and hard, the bowl containing the weighed Foundation can be put in the oven for a minute or two in order to facilitate the beating needed to restore its original creaminess.

3. SUGAR – EGGS – GROUND ALMONDS – TREACLE – JAM– MARMALADE – ORANGE OR LEMON JUICE AND GRATED PEEL

These are beaten into the creamed Cake Foundation with a fork or a wire or perforated spoon.

4. DRIED FRUIT – PRESERVED OR CRYSTALLIZED GINGER – NUTS – COCONUT – ROLLED OATS – CHOCOLATE LUMPS

These are lightly folded into the above mixture with a metal spoon.

5. FLOUR – RAISING AGENTS – SPICES – SALT – COCOA – GROUND RICE – CORNFLOUR

These should be sifted at least once. When you feel conscientious, or for extra lightness, sift three times.

For light mixtures fold the flour, etc. gently into the other ingredients with a large metal spoon.

For dough-like mixtures work it in with a palette knife or perforated spoon.

6. LIQUIDS

For light mixtures add gradually together with the flour, etc.

For dough-like mixtures, as for scones, the liquid is added after the flour has been worked into the Foundation. A palette or pliable knife is good for this job.

Cake Foundation Recipes

Should you be temporarily out of Cake Foundation and have no available time to make a fresh supply, do not despair. You can convert any of the following recipes *if they include* 10 *oz Cake Foundation* by remembering that this is equivalent to 4 *oz butter or margarine*, 4 *oz caster sugar and* 1 *egg*. Instead of the Cake Foundation add the above to all the other given ingredients.

CAKES

Standard Sponge

If Cake Foundation were only used for making Standard Sponge recipes, it would still be invaluable.

In a moment Cake Foundation becomes Standard Sponge Batter, which in turn is transformed into sponges, small cakes or puddings.

The formula is one of simple arithmetic.

Use:

any weight Cake Foundation	*liquid, sufficient to enable the*
half the same weight self-raising	*batter just to drop from the*
flour	*spoon*

The liquid can be *milk – milk and water – milk and fruit juice or squash – neat fruit juice or squash*.

However, to save even more time and effort, in some recipes weighing and arithmetic can be avoided. Bulk for bulk, Cake Foundation weighs twice as much as flour. Thus, using the same spoon for both, 1 heaped spoon of Cake Foundation weighs the same as 2 rounded spoons of flour; and for recipes in which the exact weight of the Standard Sponge Batter is not important, the formula can be:

Using the same spoon for Cake Foundation and flour:
  any number of heaped spoons Cake Foundation
  the same number rounded spoons self-raising flour

It is a good idea to keep a large tablespoon especially for this purpose, and find out how heaped or rounded it must be to scoop up 2 oz Cake Foundation or 1 oz flour respectively.

Standard Sponge Small Cakes   Oven Setting 400°F, Mark 6

Suggested Flavours

vanilla	*orange*	*chocolate*	*cinnamon*
lemon	*coffee*	*ginger*	*mixed spice*

Suggested Additions

dried fruit	*ginger, preserved*	*nuts*
glacé cherries	*or crystallized*	*caraway seeds*

Half fill small oiled foil baking cases with the mixture.
Bake 10–15 minutes in pre-heated oven.

Standard Sponge Victoria Sandwich   Oven Setting 375°F, Mark 5

Make a *Standard Sponge* (p. 142) using 10 *oz or 5 heaped tablespoons Cake Foundation and 5 oz or 5 rounded tablespoons of self-raising flour.* Turn this into two greased, floured, 8-inch sandwich tins, with $1\frac{1}{4}$–$1\frac{1}{2}$ inch straight sides. Bake in pre-heated oven about 20 minutes.

Classic Sponge

This time-honoured sponge mixture of *eggs and their weight in flour, butter and sugar,* can easily be made with Cake Foundation, i.e.

MADE WITH 2 EGGS

10 *oz Cake Foundation*
1 *egg*
4 *oz self-raising flour*

MADE WITH 3 EGGS

2 *oz butter or margarine*
10 *oz Cake Foundation*
2 *oz caster sugar*
2 *eggs*
6 *oz self-raising flour*

Cake Foundation Bun Mixture   Oven Setting 400°F, Mark 6

These buns are quite delicious when fresh, so do not make too many. The next day or so they are not nearly so nice, but still good if given a brief spell in a hot oven shortly before serving. This is another simple recipe which requires no weighing.

Using the same spoon for the Foundation and flour, allow:
3 *rounded spoons self-raising flour*
to each
2 *heaped spoons Cake Foundation*

Knead into a dough and fashion little balls. These are made into the following buns or into others of your own devising.

Bake them on a well greased baking sheet for 10 to 15 minutes in a pre-heated oven.

Raspberry Buns

Place the little balls of *Bun Mixture* on the baking sheet. Make a hole in each one with the end of a wooden spoon and fill this with *raspberry jam*.

Cornflake Cookies

These are always popular. Put some *cornflakes* into a small pudding basin. Drop each ball of *Bun Mixture* individually into the flakes. Knead lightly. Re-roll into balls so that plenty of flakes are inside as well as outside each bun. These buns can be baked as they are, or a little *raspberry jam* or *Butterscotch sauce* (p. 80) can be inserted as given for *Raspberry Buns*.

Ginger Buns

Add *a little ground ginger* to the *Bun Mixture* flour before sieving. Make one or more holes in each bun and insert *pieces of crystallized ginger*. Close up holes.

Chocolate Buns

Make holes in the balls of *Bun Mixture* and insert *a piece of chocolate* or push *several chocolate drops* into each bun. Close up the holes. When baked, cover with *Chocolate Icing* or *Chocolate Couverture* (see p. 165).

Walnut Butterscotch Buns

Place balls of *Bun Mixture* on the baking sheet and make a large hole in each with the end of a wooden spoon. Fill holes with *Butterscotch Sauce* (p. 80) and *chopped walnuts*.

Rock Cakes　　　　　　　　　　　Oven Setting 400°F, Mark 6

5 oz Cake Foundation	*4 oz plain flour*
2 oz currants	*½ teaspoon baking powder*

Put small rough heaps of the mixture on to a greased, floured sheet. Bake 10 to 15 minutes, or till brown, in pre-heated oven.

Short Cakes

1½ oz butter or margarine (warmed)	*⅛ teaspoon bicarbonate of soda*
5 oz Cake Foundation	*⅛ teaspoon of mixed spice*
4 oz currants and sultanas	*½ teaspoon vanilla* (optional)
6 oz plain flour	

Put small rough heaps of the mixture on to a greased, floured sheet. Bake 10 to 15 minutes, or till brown, in pre-heated oven.

If stale, this delicious form of Rock Cake can be rejuvenated by 10 minutes in a paper bag placed in a medium hot oven.

White Ginger Rocks   Oven Setting 400°F, Mark 6

1½ *oz butter or margarine* (warmed)   ½ *teaspoon ground ginger*
5 *oz Cake Foundation*   ½ *teaspoon ground caraway seeds*
1 *oz caster sugar*   ⅛ *teaspoon bicarbonate of soda*
6 *oz plain flour*   *A few blanched almonds*

Mix all the ingredients except the almonds.

Place the mixture in small heaps on a well-greased baking sheet with an almond on top of each heap. Bake in pre-heated oven for 10 to 15 minutes.

Small Cherry Cakes   Oven Setting 400°F, Mark 6

5 *oz Cake Foundation*   1 *oz cornflour*
2½ *oz glacé cherries, chopped*   ½ *teaspoon baking powder*
3 *oz plain flour*   *A little milk*

Oil small foil baking cases. Half fill these with the mixture. Bake for 15 to 20 minutes in pre-heated oven.

Small Chocolate Cakes   Oven Setting 400°F, Mark

1 *oz butter or margarine* (warmed)   5 *oz self-raising flour*
5 *oz Cake Foundation*   1 *oz ground rice*
1 *oz caster sugar*   3 *dessertspoons chocolate powder*
2 *oz chopped walnuts* (optional)   *A little strong coffee*

Spoon mixture into oiled, foil baking cases.

Bake for 10 to 15 minutes in pre-heated oven. When cold, cover with *Chocolate Icing* or *Chocolate Couverture* (p. 165).

Small Orange Cakes   Oven Setting 400°F, Mark 6

5 *oz Cake Foundation*   4 *oz self-raising flour*
1 *tablespoon marmalade*   *The orange juice*
Grated rind of 1 *small orange*

Spoon mixture into oiled, foil baking cases.
Bake 10 to 15 minutes in pre-heated oven.

Princess Cake
Oven Setting 325°F, Mark 3

7½ oz Cake Foundation
2 oz plain flour
1½ oz ground rice

¾ teaspoon baking powder
½ teaspoon vanilla

Put mixture into greased and floured sandwich tin 7 × 1¼ inch. Bake for 45–50 minutes in pre-heated oven. When cooked, turn out carefully, as the cake is fragile. Cool upside down. Spread with *raspberry jam* and sprinkle with *desiccated coconut*.

American Walnut Cake
Oven Setting 350°–375°F, Mark 4–5

10 oz Cake Foundation
1 egg and 1 egg yolk
A few drops of vanilla

4 oz self-raising flour
1 oz cornflour
1½ oz chopped walnuts

Put mixture either in a 6½–7 inch cake tin or two 6½–7 inch Sandwich tins, in each case well greased and floured.

Bake in pre-heated oven 55–65 minutes or 20–30 minutes.

Ice cake when cold with *American Frosting* (p. 166) and decorate with *walnuts*. When a sandwich has been made, fill with a *vanilla flavoured Butter Icing* (p. 166) before frosting.

Chocolate Mocha Cake
Oven Setting 375°F, Mark 5

10 oz Cake Foundation
4 oz caster sugar
1 egg
8 oz plain flour

2 tablespoons cocoa
2 teaspoons baking powder
3 fluid oz strong coffee
1 fluid oz milk

Turn into two greased 8 inch sandwich tins. Bake 15 to 20 minutes in pre-heated oven. When cold cover with *Coffee Icing* (p. 165) and fill with *Coffee Butter Icing* (p. 166) or Cream Garnish (p. 109). A really delicious and not extravagant cake.

Cherry, Seed and Lump of Chocolate Cakes
Oven Setting 350°F, Mark 4

These three cakes are made with the same mixture, are all nice and not too rich.

The Lump of Chocolate Cake is especially popular with children, and in our family is known as the 'This or That Cake'. After the first slice has been cut, it is a gamble as to which side will have the most chocolate – they choose their side and chance their luck.

10 *oz Cake Foundation*
1 *egg*
6 *to* 8 *oz glacé cherries*
  (see *Cherry Gateau*, below)

or 2 *tablespoons caraway seeds*
or 6 *to* 8 *oz plain chocolate,*
  cut in small pieces
6 *oz self-raising flour*
2 *tablespoons milk*

Flavouring is optional, but *lemon* in the cherry cake, *mixed spice* in the seed cake, and *vanilla* in the Lump of Chocolate may be thought an improvement. Turn the mixture into a greased, floured 7 inch tin and bake for about an hour in a pre-heated oven.

The Cherry and the Lump of Chocolate Cakes are nice when iced – with *Lemon* and *Chocolate Icing* respectively, p. 165.

Sand Cake   Oven Setting 350°F, Mark 4

1½ *oz margarine or butter* (warmed)
5 *oz Cake Foundation*
2 *oz caster sugar*
1 *egg yolk*

6 *oz cornflour*
¾ *teaspoon baking powder*
Vanilla flavouring
Lastly fold in 1 *stiffly whisked egg white*

Turn the mixture into a greased, floured 1 lb loaf tin. Bake 45 minutes to 1 hour in a pre-heated oven. This is a small cake which can well be doubled.

Ground Rice Cake   Oven Setting 350°F, Mark 4

10 *oz Cake Foundation*
1 *egg*
4 *oz ground rice*
2 *oz plain flour*

¾ *teaspoon baking powder*
A little vanilla
A little milk

Turn the mixture into a greased, floured 7 inch tin. Bake for about 1 hour in pre-heated oven.

This is a delicious cake, which lends itself to variations – different flavourings – to be iced (pp. 165–6) – cut into layers and filled with *Butter Icing* (p. 166) or *Cream Garnish* (p. 109).

Cherry Gateau   Oven Setting 350°F, Mark 4

Before mixing the ingredients, the cherries should be prepared. Put cherries in a small sieve over a basin, and pour boiling water over them. This will wash off all the surplus sugar, and prevent their sinking to the bottom of the cake. Cut the cherries into halves.

3 *oz butter or margarine* (warmed)	10 *oz plain flour*
10 *oz Cake Foundation*	3 *oz ground rice*
3 *oz caster sugar*	2 *teaspoons baking powder*
2 *eggs*	*A little milk or sherry*
½ *lb glacé cherries* (more if you like)	

Turn the mixture into a greased, floured 9 inch tin. Bake 1 to 1¼ hours in pre-heated oven. When cold, ice and decorate with cherries.

Cinnamon Cake   Oven Setting 375°F, Mark 5

2 *oz butter or margarine* (warmed)	5 *oz plain flour*
5 *oz Cake Foundation*	½ *teaspoon cream of tartar*
1 *egg*	¼ *teaspoon bicarbonate of soda*
A few chopped walnuts and sultanas	1½ *teaspoons of cinnamon*

Turn the mixture into a small greased, floured 1 lb loaf tin. Bake 30 to 40 minutes in pre-heated oven.

This makes a small cake. It's nice, so you may like to double all the ingredients.

Pain de Gênes   Oven Setting 350°F, Mark 4

This cake may be extravagant, but it is so good that every penny is well spent.

10 *oz Cake Foundation*	3 *oz plain flour*
6 *oz caster sugar*	*A liqueur glass of kirsch*
4 *eggs* beaten alternately with	(optional)
5 *oz ground almonds*	

Turn the mixture into a shallow, greased 7 inch tin with greased paper or Bakewell on the bottom. Bake for 1½ hours or longer, reducing the heat to 325°F, Mark 3, after the first 60 minutes. Leave the cake in the tin until cold before turning out.

By halving all the ingredients a smaller cake can be made. Bake this in an 8 inch sandwich tin for about an hour.

Greek Orange Cake   Oven Setting 425°F, Mark 7

This, another expensive cake is also worth the extravagance.

2 *oz butter* (warmed)	2 *eggs*
10 *oz Cake Foundation*	9 *oz fine semolina*
2 *oz sugar, caster*	3 *teaspoons baking powder*
1½ *level teaspoons grated orange rind*	4 *oz ground almonds*
5 *scant tablespoons orange juice*	

Beat together the butter, cake foundation, sugar and orange rind. Beat in the orange juice. Whip the eggs and beat in gradually. Stir in the mixed semolina, baking powder and ground almonds. Place in a well greased 9 inch ring mould 2½ inches deep. Bake in pre-heated oven for 10 minutes, then reduce heat to 350°F, Mark 4, for a further 30 minutes.

A few minutes before the cake is cooked, make the following syrup: Place in a saucepan:

6 *oz sugar*	2 *dessertspoons lemon juice*
5 *scant tablespoons water*	1½ *inch cinnamon stick or*
	½ *teaspoon powdered cinnamon*

Stir until the sugar is dissolved, then boil without stirring until the syrup begins to thicken. Add 3 *teaspoons orange juice* or *squash* and 1 *tablespoon shredded candied peel*. Boil a second time. Turn cake out on to a warm platter, and pour the hot syrup over at once.

Orange Cake   Oven Setting 350°F, Mark 4

10 *oz Cake Foundation*	2 *table spoons marmalade*
grated rind of 1 *large orange crushed*	8 *oz self-raising flour*
with	*juice of the orange*
1 *tablespoon caster sugar*	

Turn batter into a greased 2 lb loaf tin and bake for 1 hour in pre-heated oven.

Orange, Rum, Chocolate Cake

This delicious cake is suitable for any great occasion.

Orange Cake as given above	*Rich Chocolate Icing* (p. 165)
Rum Butter (p. 82)	

When the Orange Cake is cold, slice it horizontally into three, and sandwich the layers together again with two liberal spreadings of Rum Butter.

Ice with a Rich Chocolate Icing made with 6 *oz plain chocolate* and 1½ *oz butter*.

Chocolate Cake   Oven Setting 350°F, Mark 4

This is by no means an economical cake, but it is so delicious, an honest-to-goodness Chocolate Cake – no cocoa powder – moist and rich. Be warned, do not cut over-generous slices.

First prepare the chocolate. Put in a small saucepan $\frac{1}{2}$ *lb good plain chocolate*, cut into small pieces. Add 2$\frac{1}{2}$ *tablespoons milk* and $\frac{1}{2}$ *teaspoon vanilla*.

Stir over gentle heat using a wooden spoon, until the chocolate has melted and the mixture is smooth. Set this aside, and prepare the cake:

4 *oz butter* (warmed)	4 *oz plain flour*
10 *oz Cake Foundation*	2 *oz ground rice*
2 *oz caster sugar*	1 *teaspoon baking powder*
3 *eggs*	Now fold in the *melted chocolate and milk*

Turn the mixture into a well-greased 8 inch tin with greased paper or Bakewell on the bottom. Bake for 1 hour or a little longer in pre-heated oven. This cake should be baked quite ten days before it is iced and eaten.

After storing, ice with *a Rich Chocolate Icing* (p. 165), and decorate with *walnuts*.

White Sponge Ring   Oven Setting 350°F, Mark 4

This is nice, and a good way of using up left-over egg whites.

5 *oz Cake Foundation*	4 *fluid oz milk*
4 *oz caster sugar*	$\frac{1}{2}$ *teaspoon vanilla or* $\frac{1}{4}$ *teaspoon*
9 *fluid oz sifted plain flour*	*vanilla and* $\frac{1}{8}$ *teaspoon almond*
1$\frac{1}{2}$ *teaspoons baking powder*	*essence*
$\frac{1}{8}$ *teaspoon salt*	2 *egg whites*

Gradually whisk the sugar into the Cake Foundation with a wire or perforated spoon.

Add the baking powder and salt to the sifted flour and sift it twice again.

Sift one third of this flour mixture into the Cake Foundation and sugar, and whisk it in with one third of the milk. Repeat twice more, and then stir in the essence.

Whip the egg whites until stiff, but not too dry, and fold them lightly into the batter. Pour this into a very well greased 8–8$\frac{1}{2}$ inch sponge ring tin.

Bake in pre-heated oven for 45 minutes.

This cake can be iced and decorated as it is, or can first be sliced into layers and filled with jam or lemon curd or one of the *Cake Fillings* given on pp. 166–7. It can also be served as a sweet, e.g. *Peach Rum Ring*, p. 173.

Ginger Cake   Oven Setting 350°F, Mark 4

A really good cake that keeps fresh for weeks.

10 *oz Cake Foundation*	1 *oz ground ginger*
5 *fluid oz golden syrup*	1 *teaspoon mixed spice*
1 *egg*	½ *teaspoon bicarbonate of soda*
8 *oz plain flour*	1 *gill warm milk*

Turn the mixture into greased, floured 7 inch tin. Bake about 1½ hours in pre-heated oven.

Ginger Bread   Oven Setting 350°F, Mark 4

Another treat for those who like ginger. It is the type of Ginger Bread that was sold at country fairs, and from which the gilt was so easily dislodged.

5 *oz Cake Foundation*	1 *oz ground ginger*
2 *oz brown sugar*	¼ *oz caraway seed*
1 *lb warmed golden syrup*	2 *teaspoons bicarbonate of soda*
1 *egg*	5 *fluid oz hot water*
1 *lb plain flour*	

Turn the mixture into one or two well-greased meat tins. Only half fill tins. Bake 1½ hours in pre-heated oven.

Golden Cake   Oven Setting 350°F, Mark 4

This is a nice large cake that keeps fresh for some considerable time.

3 *oz butter or margarine* (warmed)	¼ *lb ground almonds*
10 *oz Cake Foundation*	1 *lb plain flour*
2 *oz caster sugar*	5 *fluid oz milk* (warmed)
5 *fluid oz golden syrup* (warmed)	¼ *teaspoon bicarbonate of soda*
1 *egg*	

Blend all the ingredients except a little of the warmed milk and the bicarbonate of soda. Dissolve the latter in the remainder of the warm milk and stir into the mixture.

Put into an 8 inch greased and floured cake tin. Bake for about 1½ hours in a pre-heated oven.

If a smaller cake is preferred, use a very small egg, and halve all the other ingredients. Place in a 2 lb loaf tin and bake for about 1¼ hours.

FRUIT CAKES

Fruit cakes are a must for most households, as not only do they complete a tea table, but a slice of nice moist fruit cake is just right for a packed lunch or a late night snack.

Thanks to packets of prepared fruit, the making of these cakes is greatly simplified. When you also have Cake Foundation, your fruit cakes are baking in next to no time. With this fact, and their popularity, in mind, we are giving recipes for a wide range of fruit cakes.

A Very Plain Fruit Cake   Oven Setting 350°F, Mark 4

A good crusty cake, just right for healthy everyday appetites.

The following ingredients are for a very small cake, but it is a simple matter to adjust this to a 7½ oz, a 10 oz or a 12½ oz Cake Foundation recipe.

5 oz Cake Foundation   *½ teaspoon baking powder*
5 oz mixed fruit   *2 tablespoons boiling milk*
4 oz plain flour

Turn the mixture into a floured, greased loaf tin – no paper needed. Bake in pre-heated oven for 1½ to 2 hours. After the first half-hour reduce heat to 325° or 300°F, Mark 3 or 2.

A Richer Fruit Cake   Oven Setting 350°F, Mark 4

10 oz Cake Foundation   *¼ teaspoon lemon essence*
1 egg   *¼ teaspoon almond essence*
8 oz mixed fruit   *½ teaspoon cinnamon*
2 oz candied peel   *8 oz self-raising flour*
¼ teaspoon vanilla

Turn the mixture into a greased, floured cake tin. Bake in pre-heated oven for 1½ to 2 hours. After the first half-hour, gradually reduce heat to 325°F, Mark 3.

A Rich Fruit Cake   Oven Setting 350°F, Mark 4

A delicious cake, suitable for any occasion, including Christmas. One advantage is that it can either be cut the day after baking or kept for some time in a tin.

The cake given is not very large; therefore double all the ingredients when a larger one is wanted.

3 *oz butter or margarine* (warmed)
5 *oz Cake Foundation*
3 *oz soft brown sugar*
1 *egg*
the grated rind of 1 *small lemon*
2 *oz raisins*
2 *oz cherries*
2 *oz candied peel*

4 *oz sultanas*
6 *oz currants*
6½ *oz plain flour*
¼ *teaspoon nutmeg*
¼ *teaspoon mixed spice*
¼ *teaspoon bicarbonate of soda*
    dissolved in a little warm milk

Turn the mixture into well-greased cake tin with greased paper on the bottom. Bake for 3 hours in pre-heated oven, the first 20 minutes at 350°F, Mark 4. Then reduce heat gradually to 300°F, Mark 2, or lower if the cake is cooking too quickly.

The Richest, Most Luscious Fruit Cake   Oven Setting 325°F, Mark 3

A cake that stands alone – all who taste it agree there is none comparable.

Suitable for weddings, Christmas, or other very special occasions.

This cake is steamed as well as baked, so before embarking on it make sure you have a pan, fish kettle or boiler large enough for your cake tin. This tin must not have a detachable bottom.

1½ *oz butter* (warmed)
10 *oz Cake Foundation*
1 *oz caster sugar*
3 *eggs*
½ *lb currants*
½ *lb raisins*
½ *lb sultanas*

¼ *lb glacé cherries*
2 *oz chopped blanched almonds*
2 *oz chopped candied peel*
5½ *oz plain flour*
½ *teaspoon mixed spice*
½ *teaspoon bicarbonate of soda*
1 *small glass sherry or brandy*

The procedure is a little different from that given for the other Cake Foundation recipes. The butter, sugar and Cake Foundation are creamed together as usual. The 3 eggs are broken into a basin and beaten with a fork. The prepared fruit and almonds are mixed together in another basin. The flour, spice and bicarbonate of soda are sieved into a third basin. Then the eggs, fruit and flour are added little by little, each in turn; first beat then stir. Lastly add the sherry or brandy.

Turn the mixture into a well-greased tin – square if possible – with greased paper or Bakewell on the bottom.

Cover the top with aluminium foil and two layers of paper. Fasten firmly with string.

C.A.—F

Stand cake in a pan of boiling water, letting the water come halfway up the tin. If the pan lid is very close fitting, fix a piece of string between the pan and its lid to make a small outlet for the steam to escape. This is to avoid a puddle forming on top of the cake.

Steam for 2½ hours. Take cake out of steamer. Remove foil and paper. Bake in pre-heated oven for 1 hour at 325°F, Mark 3.

The above recipe will make a cake of just over 3 lbs. Double all the ingredients if you should want a very large one.

This cake should be made at least a month before it is needed: six weeks is better. When wrapped in grease-proof paper and stored in an airtight tin, it will keep up to a year.

Scotch Fruit Cake   Oven Setting 350°F, Mark 4

2 *oz butter or margarine* (warmed)
10 *oz Cake Foundation*
1 *large egg*
2 *oz chopped walnuts*
4 *oz chopped dates*

2 *oz raisins*
2 *oz rolled oats*
6 *oz self-raising flour*
1 *teaspoon mixed spice*
a little milk

Turn the mixture into a greased, floured 2 lb loaf tin. Bake in pre-heated oven for 1¼ to 1½ hours.

Swedish Fruit Cake   Oven Setting 350°F, Mark 4

This is a very good and unusual fruit cake. Don't forget to steam the figs for 20 minutes, some time before mixing all the ingredients.

2 *oz butter or margarine* (warmed)
10 *oz Cake Foundation*
1 *egg*
2 *tablespoons top milk or evaporated milk*
4 *oz steamed figs*, cut up
1 *tablespoon rum or whisky*

2 *oz candied peel*, shredded
2 *oz walnuts or blanched almonds*, chopped
4 *oz sultanas*
8 *oz plain flour*
2 *teaspoons baking powder*
pinch of salt

Turn the mixture into a greased 2 lb loaf tin and bake for 1 to 1½ hours in the pre-heated oven.

Sultana Cake   Oven Setting 350°F, Mark 4

2 *oz butter or margarine* (warmed)
5 *oz Cake Foundation*
1 *oz caster sugar*
1 *egg*
¼ *lb sultanas*

1 *oz candied peel*
½ *lb plain flour*
1 *teaspoon baking powder*
2½ *fluid oz milk or sherry*

Turn mixture into a well-greased and floured 2 lb loaf tin. Bake in pre-heated oven for 1½ hours, reducing heat after first half-hour to 325°F, Mark 3.

Chocolate Sultana Cake   Oven Setting 350°F, Mark 4

2 *oz butter or margarine* (warmed)   10 *oz plain flour*
10 *oz Cake Foundation*   2 *oz ground rice*
1 *egg*   1½ *teaspoons baking powder*
6 *oz sultanas*   3 *tablespoons chocolate powder*
A little milk to mix, if necessary

Bake the mixture in a well greased and floured 2 lb loaf tin for half an hour at 350°F, Mark 4, and a further ¾–1 hour at 325°F, Mark 3.

Treacle Fruit Cake   Oven setting 350°F, Mark 4

2 *oz butter or margarine* (warmed)   2 *oz sultanas*
5 *oz Cake Foundation*   1 *oz candied peel*
1 *egg*   ½ *lb plain flour*
2 *oz golden syrup or treacle*   *teaspoon bicarbonate of soda*
3 *oz currants*   2 *tablespoons milk*

Turn the mixture into a well greased and floured 2 lb loaf tin and bake in pre-heated oven for about 1½ hours. After the first half-hour, reduce heat to 325°F, Mark 3.

Apple Sauce Cake   Oven Setting 350°F, Mark 4

A fruit cake that is different, nice and moist, with plenty of flavour and not too rich.
   After baking, the cake improves if left for a few days before cutting.

1 *oz butter or margarine* (warmed)   2 *oz chopped walnuts*
10 *oz Cake Foundation*   2 *oz preserved or crystallized ginger*
2 *oz Barbados sugar*   2 *oz candied peel*
1 *egg*   8 *oz plain flour*
½ *pint Apple Purée* (pp. 132–3)   1 *teaspoon bicarbonate of soda*
8 *oz mixed currants, sultanas and
   raisins*

Turn the mixture into a round, greased 7 inch tin with a detachable bottom which should be papered. Dredge the cake with *caster sugar*.

Bake in pre-heated oven for about 2 hours. After 45 minutes, reduce oven setting to 325°F, Mark 3, and later to 300°F, Mark 2, if necessary.

To remove cake from tin, stand it on a jam jar or basin and push down the tin's side.

SCONES

When a supply of Cake Foundation is available, it takes far less time to prepare your scones than it does to heat the oven in which to bake them.

Oven Setting 425°F, Mark 7

They are made with:

> *any weight Cake Foundation*
> *2½ times the same weight self-raising flour*
> *milk or whey* (p. 111)

However, as with *Standard Sponge* (p. 142), weighing can be avoided and the scone ingredients can be measured with a spoon.

> *For every heaped spoonful of Cake Foundation*
> *5 rounded spoonfuls (the same spoon) self-raising flour*
> *milk or whey*

1 heaped tablespoon Foundation and 5 rounded tablespoons flour should make 6 medium-sized scones.

There is no need to mess your hands, working surface or rolling pin – just work the flour into the Foundation with a fork or perforated spoon, like a kitchamajig. Then, using a palette knife or a pliable kitchen knife, mix in just enough liquid to make a moist but easily-handled dough. Turn the dough straight on to a well-floured baking sheet. Pat it out with your hands to a thickness of about ¾ inch, and cut out the scones – all on the baking sheet. Bake for 8 to 10 minutes in pre-heated oven.

Left-overs can be stored for several days in a polythene bag. Before serving, these should be put in a paper bag and heated in a hot oven for about 5 minutes.

Wholewheat Meal Scones

Make these with *wholewheat meal* instead of self-raising flour, and allow 1 *teaspoon cream of tartar* and ½ *teaspoon bicarbonate of soda* for each ½ lb of meal.

Savoury Scones   Oven Setting 400°F, Mark 6

These make a good luncheon or supper dish.

To make 2 savoury scones (1 per serving), allow:

> *Scone Dough*, made with:
> 1 *heaped tablespoon Cake Foundation*   4 *rashers bacon*
> 5 *rounded tablespoons self-raising flour*   3–4 *oz cheese*
> *milk or whey*

Divide dough into two rounds, and roll or pat these out to a thickness of about ½ inch. Cover them with bacon and top with slices of cheese, about ¼ inch thick.

Bake in pre-heated oven for 15 minutes or until the dough is cooked and the cheese has melted and is beginning to brown.

If preferred, one large scone can be made and, when baked, cut into portions.

BISCUITS

Cake Foundation lends itself splendidly to many classic biscuit recipes which can usually be made in half the given quantities. This is an advantage as it allows for greater variety and the saving of time. Most of the following recipes are adapted, though some have been contrived especially for Cake Foundation.

Biscuits are ideal for Cooking Ahead, as they are such excellent tin dwellers. When time permits, a selection of favourites can be made, packed in not too large tins, sealed with sellotape to keep fresh, if needed, for months. Really good biscuits are very costly to buy, therefore it is most gratifying to have a stock of your own baking.

Most biscuit recipes instruct that the dough should be rolled out and cut into shapes – a time-consuming process. In a number of the following recipes this chore can be avoided by rolling small pieces of dough into balls by hand. These are placed on the greased baking sheet and pressed into rounds. This is far quicker, though the result may not be quite so fancy! Then there are the biscuits made from softer doughs, like the *Ice Box Cookies*, and those that can be dropped from a spoon directly on to the baking sheet.

Somerset Crisps   Oven Setting 400°F, Mark 6

1½ *oz butter or margarine* (warmed)   1½ *oz caster sugar*
4 *oz Cake Foundation*   6½ *oz self-raising flour*

FLAVOURING:

the choice of:

½ teaspoon of ground ginger,	or ½ teaspoon vanilla
cinnamon or	or a few drops almond essence
mixed spice	or orange or lemon flavourings
	(p. 167)

Knead the mixture into a dough. Either roll out fairly thinly and cut into shapes, or form little balls by hand and flatten these on the greased baking sheet.

Bake 10–15 minutes in pre-heated oven.

Almond Biscuits   Oven setting 400°F, Mark 6

5 oz Cake Foundation	¼ lb plain flour
2 oz ground almonds	

Knead the mixture into a dough. Either roll out fairly thinly and cut into shapes, or form little balls by hand and flatten these on the greased baking sheet.

Bake 10–15 minutes in pre-heated oven.

Vienna Biscuits   Oven Setting 400°F, Mark 6

5 oz Cake Foundation	⅛ teaspoon bicarbonate of soda
2 oz caster sugar	¼ teaspoon cinnamon
3½ oz plain flour	A very little milk
¾ teaspoon cream of tartar	

Knead into a dough, and roll out thinly. Cut into rounds or fancy shapes – on the small side, as these biscuits spread considerably.

Place, not too closely, on a greased baking sheet. Bake about 10 minutes in pre-heated oven.

These make good chocolate biscuits if covered when cold with *Chocolate Couverture* (p. 165–6).

Great-Grandmother's Chocolate Biscuits   Oven Setting 400°F, Mark 6

A crisp biscuit with a delicious flavour.

5 oz Cake Foundation	1 oz ground almonds
2 oz bar of chocolate,	4 oz plain flour
finely grated	pinch of mixed spice

Roll dough to a thickness of $\frac{1}{4}$ inch and cut into fancy shapes, or roll into little balls and flatten on the greased baking sheet to the same thickness. Either brush with *white of egg* and decorate with *split blanched almonds* before baking, or cover with *Chocolate Couverture* (pp. 165–6) when cold after baking. Bake in pre-heated oven on a lightly greased sheet for about 15 minutes or until a nice pale brown.

Coffee Cream Biscuits   Oven Setting 375°F, Mark 5

1 *oz butter or margarine* (warmed)
5 *oz Cake Foundation*
3 *oz plain flour*

1 *oz cornflour*
2 *teaspoons Instant Coffee*

Drop heaps of the blended mixture from a teaspoon on to a baking sheet covered with Bakewell paper. The heaps must not be too close together. Smooth and shape them with a knife into rounds.

Bake in pre-heated oven for about 10 minutes.

When cold, sandwich biscuits together in pairs with *Coffee Butter Icing* (p. 166) or *Chocolate Couverture* (pp. 165–6).

Shrewsbury Biscuits   Oven Setting 325°F, Mark 3

5 *oz Cake Foundation*
$\frac{1}{2}$ *teaspoon caraway seeds* (optional)

3 *oz plain flour*
$\frac{1}{4}$ *teaspoon cinnamon*

Knead the mixture well. Either roll out and cut into rounds, or form into little balls and flatten into rounds on the greased sheet.

Bake in pre-heated oven for about 30 minutes.

Continental Sugar Biscuits   Oven Setting 400°F, Mark 6

2 *oz butter or margarine* (warmed)
5 *oz Cake Foundation*
2 *oz caster sugar*
grated rind of 1 *lemon*

1 *oz ground almonds*
$\frac{1}{2}$ *lb plain flour*
a little *vanilla*

Knead the mixture and roll out thinly. Cut into biscuits. Bake on well-greased sheet in pre-heated oven for about 10 minutes.

These biscuits, when cold, are good covered with *Chocolate Couverture* (pp. 165–6).

Shortbread   Oven setting 325°F, Mark 3

4 *oz butter* (warmed)
10 *oz Cake Foundation*

1 *lb plain flour*

Knead the dough and roll out about ⅛ inch thick. Cut into squares. Pinch edges and prick centres with a fork. Bake in pre-heated oven for about 30 minutes or until a pale brown.

Shortbread Biscuits   Oven Setting 350°F, Mark 4

2 *oz butter* (warmed)   ½ *lb plain flour*
5 *oz Cake Foundation*

Knead the dough and roll out about ⅛ inch thick. Cut into biscuits. Bake in pre-heated oven for about 20 minutes or until a pale brown.
     Whilst still hot, dip biscuits in *caster sugar*.

German Shortbread   Oven Setting 375°F, Mark 5

7½ *oz Cake Foundation*   ¾ *teaspoon baking powder*
6 *oz plain flour*   *a little milk* (if necessary)

THE FILLING

dried fruit, including chopped dates,   or *any of the sweet fillings* (pp.
     glace cherries and nuts   71–3)

Knead mixture into a dough and divide into two. Roll each piece to fit a greased 8 inch sandwich tin. Line this with one of the pieces and spread with the chosen filling. Cover with the remaining dough. Bake for about 15 to 20 minutes, or until brown, in pre-heated oven. When cooked, cut into sections, but do not turn out till nearly cold.

Cinnamon Sticks   Oven Setting 350°F, Mark 4

2 *oz butter or margarine* (warmed)   8½ *oz plain flour*
10 *oz Cake Foundation*   8 *oz cornflour*
2 *oz caster sugar*   2 *teaspoons cinnamon*
1 *egg and* 1 *egg yolk*

Knead into a dough and roll out to a thickness of about ½ inch. Cut into sticks, 3 to 4 inches long, ⅜ inch wide. Place these on a greased sheet. If you have a biscuit press, the sticks can be formed directly on the sheet. Bake in a pre-heated oven for about 1 hour.
     These ingredients make a large batch of biscuits, but this is an advantage, as they are really good and keep deliciously crunchy for a long time in an airtight tin.

Gingersnaps Oven Setting 375°F, Mark 5

These crisp spicey biscuits taste as much of cloves as they do of ginger; those who think too much so, should reduce the cloves and perhaps increase the ginger.

1 *oz butter* (warmed)	¼ *lb plain flour*
5 *oz Cake Foundation*	1 *teaspoon baking powder*
1 *oz caster sugar*	1 *teaspoon ground ginger*
2½ *tablespoons black treacle*	½–1 *teaspoon ground cloves*
1 *egg*	1 *teaspoon cinnamon*

Mix all the ingredients.

Using two teaspoons, drop little lumps of the biscuit dough into a small bowl of caster sugar. Still using the spoons, roll them in the sugar and gently form them into balls. Place these, about 3 inches apart, on baking sheets covered with Bakewell.

Bake about 15 minutes in pre-heated oven.

Gingersnaps are used in *Ginger Delights*, a delicious sweet given on p. 195.

Lemon Sugar Biscuits Oven Setting 350°F, Mark 4

5 *oz Cake Foundation*	3 *oz plain flour*
2 *oz caster sugar*	½ *teaspoon baking powder*
1 *teaspoon grated lemon rind*	2 *tablespoons lemon juice*

Mix all the ingredients.

Drop small portions of the soft dough on to baking sheets covered with Bakewell, leaving at least 3 inches between each.

Bake 15–20 minutes in pre-heated oven.

When cooked and just beginning to cool, lift biscuits with a palette or pliable knife, and, before placing them on a wire tray, slip them into a small bowl of granulated sugar, so that both sides are coated.

Honey Wholewheat Biscuits Oven Setting 400°F, Mark 6

1½ *oz butter or margarine* (warmed)	2 *tablespoons honey*
5 *oz Cake Foundation*	8 *oz wholewheat meal*

Knead dough. Roll out and cut into biscuits. Place on a baking sheet, either covered with Bakewell or well greased.

Bake for 8 to 10 minutes in pre-heated oven.

Oatmeal Biscuits   Oven Setting 400°F, Mark 6

5 *oz Cake Foundation*   ½ *pint rolled oats*
1 *oz Barbados or moist dark*   ½ *teaspoon cinnamon* (optional)
   sugar   ½ *teaspoon vanilla*

Drop heaps of the blended mixture from a teaspoon on to a baking sheet covered with Bakewell paper. The heaps must not be too close together. Smooth and shape them with a knife into rounds.

Bake in pre-heated oven for 10 minutes. Allow to cool a little before lifting the biscuits with a knife or slice and placing on a wire tray.

These are good as they are, but something special when pairs are sandwiched together with *Rum Butter* (p. 82).

Flap Jacks   Oven Setting 350°F, Mark 4

These are not as sticky as the orthodox Flap Jack and they always remain crunchy.

2½ *oz butter or margarine* (warmed)   2¾ *oz wholemeal flour*
5 *oz Cake Foundation*   3 *oz rolled oats*
2 *oz Demerara sugar*   ½ *teaspoon bicarbonate of soda*

Spread the mixture evenly in a greased Swiss roll tin about 11 by 7 inches.

Bake for 20 to 30 minutes in pre-heated oven.

Cut immediately into small squares or fingers, but do not remove from the tin until cold.

Stuffed Monkey   Oven Setting 375°F, Mark 5

This unusual but delectable sweetmeat is not really a biscuit, but finds its way here as it can be made with Cake Foundation and is a most successful tin dweller.

THE 'MONKEY'

2 *oz butter or margarine* (warmed)   9 *oz plain flour*
10 *oz Cake Foundation*   ½ *teaspoon cinnamon*
2 *oz Demerara sugar*

THE STUFFING

4 *oz ground almonds*   1½ *oz melted butter or*
8 *oz shredded candied peel*   *margarine*
  (see p. 168)   1 *egg yolk*
                                       ½ *teaspoon vanilla*

THE TOPPING

Egg white   Demerara sugar

Mix the 'monkey' ingredients into a pliable dough. Knead it and divide into two. Roll two similar rectangles about ⅛ inch thick. (Should the dough be too soft to handle easily, chill it for a while.)

Blend together the stuffing ingredients, spread the mixture over one of the dough rectangles and cover it with the other. Roll it lightly to make firm. Brush over with egg white and sprinkle with sugar. Cut into squares or triangles and place these, not too close together, on a baking sheet. Bake in pre-heated oven for 20–30 minutes until the 'monkeys' are a nice golden brown.

ICE BOX COOKIES

This is a good way of treating softer doughs.

Having made the dough according to the recipe, chill it for a while in the refrigerator. When firm enough to handle, form into a roll, about 2 inches in diameter. Wrap this in waxed or grease-proof paper, and leave in the freezing compartment for about 24 hours.

The next day, when the dough is hard and thoroughly chilled, cut into slices, as thin as possible, and place on a baking sheet covered with Bakewell, or brushed liberally with olive oil. Bake according to recipe.

Vanilla Ice Box Cookies   Oven Setting 350°F, Mark 4

   5 oz Cake Foundation   ⅛ *teaspoon salt*
   2 oz caster sugar   1 *teaspoon baking powder*
   3½ oz plain flour   ½ *teaspoon vanilla*

Follow *Ice Box Cooky* directions given above.

Bake 15 to 20 minutes in pre-heated oven.

These biscuits are good sandwiched together in pairs with *Chocolate Couverture* (pp. 165–6) both between and on top. They are also good served with ice cream in place of wafers.

Ginger Ice Box Cookies   Oven Setting 400°F, Mark 6

   5 oz Cake Foundation   ¼ *teaspoon bicarbonate of soda*
   1 fluid oz black treacle   ¼ *teaspoon salt*
   4 oz plain flour   ¾ *teaspoon ground ginger*

Follow *Ice Box Cooky* directions given above.

Bake about 10 minutes in pre-heated oven.

Honey Ice Box Cookies   Oven Setting 375°F, Mark 5

> 5 *oz Cake Foundation*   2¾ *oz plain flour*
> 3 *teaspoons honey*   1¼ *oz cornflour*
> 1½ *oz crushed cornflakes*   1¼ *oz chopped nuts*

Follow *Ice Box Cooky* directions (p. 163).
Bake for about 10 minutes in pre-heated oven.

COCKTAIL BISCUITS

These keep well in a tin and make tasty little tit-bits to serve with
drinks.

Cheese Nibbles   Oven Setting 350°F, Mark 4

> 1 *oz butter or margarine* (warmed)   ¼ *teaspoon salt*
> 2 *oz Cake Foundation*   *pepper to taste*
> 2 *oz finely grated cheese*   *a pinch of cayenne*
>   (*Cheddar type*)   2 *oz plain flour*
> 1 *tablespoon finely grated parmesan*

Chill the prepared dough until firm enough to handle.
Then form it into a roll about 1¼ inches in diameter and wrap it in
waxed or grease-proof paper, and leave in the freezing compartment for
about 24 hours.
The next day, when the dough is hard and thoroughly chilled, cut
into slices – as thin as possible – and place on a cold greased baking
sheet.
Bake in pre-heated oven for 10 to 15 minutes.

Peanut Nibbles   Oven Setting 350°F, Mark 4

These are delicious and unusual. The salted peanuts are easily ground
in an electric grinder or liquidizer or passed through the fine disc of a
hand shredder or mincer.

> 1 *oz butter or margarine* (warmed)   ¼ *teaspoon salt*
> 2 *oz Cake Foundation*   *pepper to taste*
> 4 *oz ground salted peanuts*   *a pinch of cayenne*
>   (not too finely)   2 *oz plain flour*
> 1 *tablespoon finely grated parmesan*

Knead the dough and either roll it out thinly, cut into small shapes
and place on a baking sheet, or form the dough by hand into little balls,

place these on the baking sheet and flatten them with your hands, or the bottom of a floured milk bottle.

Bake for 10 to 15 minutes in pre-heated oven.

ICINGS, FILLINGS, FLAVOURING, ACCESSORIES

Water Icing

This is the simplest and quickest way of icing cakes and is made with:

> *icing sugar*   *very little boiling water*
> *or boiling lemon or orange juice or squash*

Contrary to the advice given in many cook books, with water icing, the sieving of the sugar is unnecessary.

Put the icing sugar in a basin and slowly add very little of the chosen boiling liquid, stirring with a wooden spoon until any lumps have disappeared. Should the icing be too thick, which is likely, add more of the liquid, literally drop by drop, until the correct consistency is obtained.

When using boiling water, flavour can be introduced by:

> *a little vanilla essence, or Camp Coffee, or a few drops of lemon or orange essence*

Chocolate Water Icing

The same as above, except that:

> *chocolate powder* and *a knob of butter or margarine* or
> *Chocolate Sauce* 2 (pp. 80–1)

are added to the icing sugar before the boiling water is introduced.

A Rich Chocolate Icing

> ½ *lb plain chocolate*   2 *oz salt-free butter*

Break the chocolate into small pieces into a pudding basin over a saucepan of boiling water. When it has melted, beat in the butter. Use the icing at once.

Chocolate Couverture

This covering chocolate can be bought loose, cut from large slabs, which is the cheapest way of buying it (packets of couverture are also on sale). This form of chocolate is excellent for covering cakes and biscuits and can also be used as a biscuit filling. Melt it as given for the chocolate in *Rich Chocolate Icing*. If there is any left over in the basin, leave it where it is to be melted with the next lot of couverture.

American Frosting

1 *egg white*	5 *tablespoons water*
8 *oz granulated sugar*	*a little vanilla essence*

Whisk the white until very stiff, either with a rotary or hand electric whisk in a pudding basin or in an electric mixer. Heat the sugar and water slowly in a small saucepan, stirring until the sugar has dissolved. Then raise heat and allow to boil without stirring until the syrup has reached a temperature of 240–45°F (a sugar thermometer is necessary). Gradually add the syrup to the egg white, while continuing the whisking. When all the syrup is incorporated, add a few drops of vanilla and do not stop whisking until the frosting is firm enough to use.

Royal Icing

To ice a small cake allow:

1 *egg white*	1 *teaspoon lemon juice*
½ *lb icing sugar*, sieved	

Put the egg white into a basin, gradually add the sugar and beat it in with a wooden spoon.

Continue the beating until the mixture is very smooth and a brilliant white – then add the lemon juice.

Cover cake with the icing, smoothing with a knife dipped in cold water.

Butter Icing

To each 1 *oz butter or margarine*
allow 1½ *oz icing sugar*

When the sugar is really lumpy, it must be sieved, but with only small lumps in fresh packets of sugar, sieving may be avoided.

All but melt the fat. Slowly add the sugar, beating all the time with a wooden spoon. The minor lumps will vanish. Add flavouring: *a little vanilla essence, Camp Coffee or Lemon or Orange flavouring* (p. 167).

Butter Icings can either be spread over cakes or used as fillings.

Chocolate and Butterscotch Butter Icings and Fillings

Make a *Butter Icing*, using about half the amount of sugar, and substitute *Chocolate Sauce* 1 *or* 2, or *Butterscotch Sauce* (pp. 79, 80).

Butterscotch Sauce Icing and Fillings

Butterscotch Sauce (p. 80) spread on top of cakes and covered with *walnuts* or *chopped almonds* or *hazel nuts* makes a welcome change from the usual icings. This sauce also provides a delicious filling for cakes and biscuits. For this it can be used as it is, or mixed with *chopped nuts and dates*.

Rum Butter (p. 82)

This makes an excellent filling for cakes and biscuits, providing these are not over rich.

Cream Garnish, pp. 109–110

Almond Icing

To cover a 3 lb cake, allow:

¾ *lb ground almonds*	9 *oz icing sugar,* sieved
9 *oz caster sugar*	2 *egg whites*

Put all the ingredients in a mixing bowl. First work them together with a wooden spoon, then knead by hand till smooth and pliable.

Lemon and Orange Flavouring

The three most popular flavours for cakes, biscuits and sweets must be vanilla, lemon and orange.

Whereas the first is entirely satisfactory in the form of bottled essence, the same cannot be said for the last two – the fresh fruit is better every time. Thus, it does seem a pity when using the juice only, to waste the good rinds, seeing these can so easily be preserved for future use. This is how it is done:

Being careful not to use the white pith, grate off the rind on to a plate. Add about the same quantity of *granulated sugar*, and crush the two together with the back of a metal spoon until the sugar is also coloured. Store in a screw-topped jar.

It keeps for months and, as well as being handy for cakes, etc., is also good in icings and fillings.

Glacé Cherries in cakes

The surplus sugar must be removed from the cherries to prevent them from sinking to the bottom of a cake.

To do this, place cherries in a small sieve over a basin and pour boiling water over them. The cherries should then be cut in halves before they are added to the cake batter.

Candied Grapefruit Peel

This is an excellent substitute for the commercial candied peel and also a splendid way of using peel which would otherwise be thrown away.

Any number of half grapefruit skins
Syrup made from sugar and water in equal parts

Soak peel in a large pan for about 36 hours, changing water two or three times. Drain.

Boil in salted water for about 25 minutes. Drain.

Boil in plain water for about 30 minutes – the peel should now be soft but not mushy. Drain and return to pan.

Prepare a syrup of sugar and water with a ratio of 1 pint of water to every pound of sugar. Pour syrup over peel. There must be sufficient syrup completely to cover the peel in the pan. Bring to boil, then reduce heat to simmering point. Repeat this procedure now and then until all the syrup has been absorbed in the peel. This may take about 4 hours. Move the peel around during the last 15 minutes to avoid risk of burning.

Remove peel and lay it on sheets of greaseproof paper which have been liberally covered with sugar. Sift over more sugar and leave for several hours to dry out. Turn peel occasionally.

When quite dry, store in air-tight containers.

This recipe may appear rather lengthy, but the end product is well worth the trouble if time and peel are available.

PUDDINGS AND SWEETS

Treacle Sponge Pudding   Oven Setting 375°F, Mark 5

For each portion allow about:
    ¼ *oz butter or margarine*   1 *tablespoon golden syrup*
    1 *tablespoon brown sugar*   3 *oz Standard Sponge* (p. 142)
                                        (2 oz Cake Foundation, 1 oz
                                        self-raising flour)

Cut the fat into small pieces and place in an oven dish, preferably rectangular. Heat this in the oven until the bottom of the dish is covered with melted fat. Add a layer of sugar and then a layer of syrup. Cover with the Standard Sponge.

Bake in pre-heated oven for 20 minutes or until sponge is cooked.

To serve, either turn the sponge on to a heated dish, or cut into squares and serve in individual portions. In both cases, be sure that the delicious toffee-like base is on top. If liked, a little *whipped cream* (p. 105, *custard* (p. 113) or a *Hard Sauce* (p. 82) can be added. However, some people may consider this pudding too rich as it is: in that case, the fat and sugar can be omitted, the syrup increased to 2 tablespoons per portion, and 1 table spoon of water added.

Note: All baked sponge puddings can be reheated, by first sprinkling with a liquid appropriate to the sponge flavour – e.g. *milk, coffee, fruit juices, alcohol* – before they are wrapped in Look and given a short spell in the oven.

Apple Sponge Pudding   Oven Setting 375°F, Mark 5

For each portion allow about:

$\frac{1}{4}$ *oz butter or margarine*
2 *tablespoons sugar – granulated or Demerara*

1 *small or $\frac{1}{2}$ a large cooking apple*, peeled, cored and sliced
3 *oz Standard Sponge* (p. 142)
(2 oz Cake Foundation, 1 oz self-raising flour)

Cut the fat into small pieces and place in an oven dish, preferably rectangular. Heat this in the oven until the bottom of the dish is covered with the melted fat.

Sprinkle half the sugar on top of the fat, then add the apples and a layer of the remaining sugar. Cover with the Standard Sponge.

Bake in pre-heated oven for about 20 minutes or until sponge is cooked.

To serve, either turn pudding on to a heated dish, or cut into squares and serve in individual portions. In both cases see that the apple is on top. This pudding is good served with *whipped cream, custard*, a *Hard Sauce* (p. 82), *or a hot Fruit Syrup* (pp. 83–4).

To reheat, see note on this page.

Fruit Sponge Puddings

These are made as given for *Apple Sponge Pudding*, except that the apple is substituted by any *fresh or bottled fruit*). It is also excellent with *rhubarb*.

Jam or Marnalade Sponge Pudding　　　Oven Setting 375°F, Mark 5

For each portion allow about:

3 *oz Standard Sponge* (p. 142)　　2½ *tablespoons jam or marmalade*
(2 oz Cake Foundation,　　　　　　1 *tablespoon water*
1 oz self-raising flour)

When preparing the Standard Sponge, add about a quarter of the jam to the Cake Foundation, before incorporating the flour and liquid.

Cover the bottom of a greased oven dish, preferably rectangular, with the rest of the jam and the water. Add the Standard Sponge.

Bake in pre-heated oven for 20 minutes or until brown.

To serve, either turn the pudding on to a hot dish, or cut into squares and serve in individual portions. In both cases, cover with the jam or marmalade sauce.

To reheat, see note on p. 169.

Chocolate, Butterscotch, Spice or　　　Oven Setting 375°F, Mark 5
Lemon Sponge Puddings

For each portion allow about:

3 *oz Standard Sponge* (p. 142)
(2 oz Cake Foundation, 1 oz self-raising flour)
either 1 *teaspoon cocoa* and 1½ *tablespoons Chocolate Sauce* 2 (p. 80)
or ½ *teaspoon vanilla* and 1½ *tablespoons Butterscotch Sauce* (p. 80)
or ½ *teaspoon mixed spice* and 1½ *tablespoons Spice Sauce* (p. 81)
or *lemon squash* and 1½ *tablespoons Lemon Filling* (p. 71)
(as the Standard Sponge liquid)

When preparing the Standard Sponge batter, incorporate either the cocoa, vanilla, mixed spice or lemon squash.

Cover the bottom of a well greased oven dish, preferably rectangular, with the sauce appertaining to the flavour, and add the Standard Sponge.

To serve, either turn the pudding on to a hot dish, or cut into squares and serve in individual portions. In both cases cover with the sauce.

To reheat, see note on p. 169.

Pineapple Plaisance   Oven Setting 375°F, Mark 5

4½ inch foil dishes are needed for this very popular recipe.

For each portion allow:

a knob of butter or margarine	*pineapple syrup*
1 *tablespoon granulated sugar*	*a little rum, sherry or orange liqueur*
1 *slice tinned pineapple*	(optional)
2 *glacé cherries,* chopped	*about* 3 *oz Standard Sponge* (p. 142)
	(2 oz Cake Foundation, 1 oz self-raising flour, using pineapple syrup instead of milk)

Place a knob of butter or margarine in each dish and melt it in the oven.

Cover the fat with sugar and place a slice of pineapple on top. Fill the hole with the cherries. Pour over a little pineapple syrup, laced, if liked, with alcohol. Cover the pineapple with the Standard Sponge.

Bake in pre-heated oven 10 to 15 minutes.

Serve hot with the pineapple on top and, if liked, with *whipped cream* (p. 105) *or a Hard Sauce* (p. 82).

Orange Delights   Oven Setting 400°F, Mark 6

This delicious sweet, when it includes alcohol, will grace any party menu, and without this extravagance it is cheap enough to be enjoyed every day. You need little foil baking cases.

For 2 Orange Delights allow:

About 3 *oz Standard Sponge* (p. 142)	2 *orange slices, cut horizontally,* pips and pith removed.
(2 oz Cake Foundation,	
1 oz self-raising flour)	2 *slices of Ice Cream* (p. 190)
4 *tablespoons orange juice*	*Whipped Cream* (p. 105)
1 *tablespoon orange liqueur, rum or brandy* (optional)	

Orange Delights are much nicer eaten fresh. Shortly before serving, half fill the oiled cases with the Standard Sponge batter and bake 10–15 minutes in pre-heated oven.

Cool and split each cake in half. Put the bottom, split side upper-most, in an individual serving bowl. Mix the alcohol, if used, with the orange juice, and pour half of it over the cake. Place the orange slices on top, then the ice cream. Cover with the remaining half cake, pour over the rest of the liquid. Top the lot with whipped cream and serve immediately.

Strawberry and Raspberry Delights

These are made the same way as *Orange Delights*, except *sherry* is used instead of the orange juice and spirit, *crushed fruit* instead of the orange slices, and *whole strawberries or raspberries* are piled on top of the whipped cream.

Strawberry and Raspberry Shortcake   Oven Setting 400°F, Mark 6

A simple and delicious Cake Foundation version of a classic favourite from the U.S.A.

To serve 4–5
For the Dough allow:

5 *oz Cake Foundation*	2½ *teaspoons baking powder*
7½ *oz plain flour*	2½ *fluid oz milk*
2½ *teaspoons corn flour*	

Also allow:

1 *lb strawberries or raspberries*	¼ *pint whipping cream* (p. 105)
Sugar to taste	

Mix and knead the dough and press it into a greased 8 inch sandwich tin.

Bake 10–12 minutes in pre-heated oven.

When cooked, immediately split short-cake in half.

Crush about ¾ of the fruit with a fork and mix in the sugar.

When the steam has escaped, sandwich the cake halves together with the crushed fruit filling. Just before serving, top with whipped cream and decorate with the remaining fruit.

Peach Rum Ring Oven Setting 375°F, Mark 5

This is a delicious and attractive looking sweet for a dinner party.

To serve 8 allow:

Classic Sponge Batter (p. 143) 2 *tablespoons orange juice*
(made with 2 eggs) 3 *tablespoons rum*
or a White Sponge Ring (p. 150) *whipped cream* (p. 105)
a large tin sliced peaches

Pour batter into well greased and floured 9 inch sponge ring mould or cake tin. Bake in pre-heated oven for 30 minutes.

Turn out on to a wire cake tray to cool. If you are using a cake tin, cut out the centre of the sponge so as to form a large ring.

Strain the peaches over a basin. To the syrup add the orange juice and rum. Stir well before pouring about ¾ of it over the sponge.

Place the peaches in the centre of the ring and pour the remainder of the syrup over. Before serving, decorate with whipped cream.

Sponge Flans Oven Setting 375°F, Mark 5

These are delicious filled with fresh fruit and cream or with tinned fruit and jelly. They are quickly prepared in greased and floured flan tins with either

Standard Sponge (p. 140)
or
Classic Sponge (p. 143)
Bake in pre-heated oven for 20 to 25 minutes.

Biba's Apple Pudding Oven Setting 375°F, Mark 5

A nice sweet of Danish origin.

To serve 6–8 allow:
10 *oz Cake Foundation* 2 *oz raisins or sultanas*
8 *oz self-raising flour* 1 *oz chopped nuts*
¼ *teaspoon salt* 2 *dessertspoons brown sugar*
12 *oz cooking apples* ½ *teaspoon powdered ginger or cinnamon*

Blend the Cake Foundation, flour and salt, and spread two thirds of the mixture on the bottom of a well greased 8 to 9 inch shallow cake tin with a loose bottom.

Peel and core the apples and cut them up thinly.

Mix together the dried fruit, nuts, sugar and spice.

Place on the batter alternate layers of apple and the dried fruit mixture, and put on top spoonfuls of the remaining batter.

Bake in pre-heated oven for 45 to 50 minutes. Serve hot or cold. It is good with whipped cream (p. 105).

Apple Cheese Pudding   Oven Setting 375°F, Mark 5

A nice, quickly made, unusual sweet.

To serve 4 to 5 allow:

A Scone Dough (p. 156,
   using 2 *tablespoons*
   Cake Foundation)
2 *oz finely grated cheese,*
   preferably Cheddar

1 *large cooking apple,*
   peeled, cored and sliced
4 *tablespoons brown sugar*
½ *oz butter or margarine*

Put the dough on a floured baking sheet in the centre of an 8 inch flan ring. Press out the dough to fit the ring.

Cover with the cheese, then lay on the apple, overlapping the slices. Sprinkle these with the sugar and dot with small pieces of butter or margarine.

Bake about 35 minutes in pre-heated oven.

Serve hot with cream (p. 105).

Apple Shortcake   Oven Setting 375°F, Mark 5

To serve 4–5 allow:

10 *oz Cake Foundation*
6 *oz self-raising flour*

½ *teaspoon cinnamon* (optional)
6 *tablespoons Apple Purée* (pp. 132–3)
   additional sugar, if needed

Make a dough with the Foundation, flour and cinnamon and divide this into two equal portions.

Press one half into a greased 7 inch loose-bottomed cake tin.

Cover with the sweetened Apple Purée.

Place the second half of the dough on a floured piece of grease-proof paper and pat it into a 7 inch diameter round.

Fit this into the tin on top of the apple and prick well with a fork.

Bake in pre-heated oven for 45 to 60 minutes.

Serve cold with cream or custard.

Swedish Apple Pudding

Oven Setting 325°F, Mark 3

To serve 4–5 allow:

2 *oz butter or margarine* (warmed)   ½ *to* ¾ *pint sweetened Apple*
5 *oz Cake Foundation*   *Purée* (pp. 132–3)
6 *oz self-raising flour*   *or Apple Compôte* (p. 134)

Make a dough with the fat, Cake Foundation and flour, and divide it into three.

Brush a 7 inch loose bottomed cake tin with oil.

Roll out the three portions of dough on well floured grease-proof paper into rounds corresponding to the size of the tin.

Place one of these on the tin bottom. Cover with half the apple. Place on this another round of the dough, then the rest of the apple, and finally the third round of dough.

This dough is very short and will probably break. Piece it together as best you can – it will join up in the cooking.

Bake in pre-heated oven for 1 hour, but lower the heat to 300°F, Mark 2, after the first half-hour.

Serve hot with *cream, custard,* or a *Hard Sauce* (p. 82), or cold with *cream* or *custard* (pp. 105, 113).

Cape Town Apple Tart

Oven Setting 375°F, Mark 5

To serve 5–6 allow:

10 *oz Cake Foundation*   1 *teaspoon vanilla*
½ *pint plain flour*   ½ *pint Apple Purée* (p. 132)
2 *teaspoons baking powder*   or *Apple Compôt* (p. 134)

Make a dough with the Cake Foundation, the flour sifted with the baking powder and the vanilla.

Press three quarters of the mixture into a greased 8 or 9 inch cake tin with a loose bottom.

Fill with the apple and dot with the remainder of the dough.

Bake in pre-heated oven for 30 to 40 minutes until a golden brown.

Serve hot with *cream, custard* or a *Hard Sauce* (p. 82) or cold with *cream* or *custard* (pp. 105, 113).

Copenhagen Fruit Pie

Oven Setting 350°F, Mark 4

To serve 4–5 allow:

stewed or bottled fruit   ¼ *teaspoon salt*
5 *oz Cake Foundation*   ½ *teaspoon bicarbonate of soda*
3 *egg yolks*   12 *fluid oz milk*
1½ *oz plain flour*   3 *well whisked egg whites*

Place in an oven dish a good layer of fruit with very little juice.

Put the Foundation in a basin and beat in the egg yolks.

Sieve together the flour, salt and bicarbonate, and stir this into the mixture. When well blended, gradually stir in the milk.

Finally fold in the whisked egg whites and pour the batter over the fruit.

Bake ¾ hour in pre-heated oven.

This pudding is nice served hot, but even better cold, when the custard which forms between the fruit and the spongy crust becomes thicker and creamier.

Lemon Meringue Pudding   Oven Setting 350°F, Mark 4

To serve 2–3 allow:

Crustless bread slices, ½ inch thick	grated rind and ju ce of 1 lemon
milk	2 whisked egg whites
5 oz Cake Foundation	caster sugar
2 egg yolks	

Cover the bottom of a shallow greased oven dish with bread slices.

Pour milk over these, enough to be absorbed.

Put the Foundation in a basin and beat in the yolks and lemon rind and juice. Fold in about ¾ of the whisked egg whites and spoon the mixture over the soaked bread. Cover with the remaining egg white, and sprinkle with sugar.

Bake in pre-heated oven for 15–20 minutes, until slightly brown.

Serve hot or cold.

This pudding can also be cooked with other dishes in an ultra-slow oven for about 8 hours.

Orange Meringue Pudding   Oven Setting 350°F, Mark 4

This is the same as *Lemon Meringue Pudding*, except the grated rind and juice of an orange is substituted for that of the lemon.

Cake Foundation Pastry   Oven Setting 375°F, Mark 5

Cake Foundation can be used as a base for a nice crisp short crust pastry. Of all the pastry doughs, this is the quickest to prepare. Using the same spoon for both ingredients, allow:

2 *rounded spoonfuls of self-raising flour to each heaped spoonful of Cake Foundation.*

Work the Foundation into the flour with a wire or perforated spoon. Knead the mixture well, if necessary sifting in a little extra flour.

As the dough is very short and brittle, it will be found easier to handle if rolled out on a piece of floured greaseproof paper.

Cake Foundation Pastry can be used for all sweet dishes that require a short crust dough, and is especially good in the three following recipes and in *Steamed Fruit Puddings* (see p. 179).

Cake Foundation Pastry Flans   Oven Setting 375°F, Mark 5

Made in well-greased and floured flan tins of any size, these are excellent and very useful. They can either be made shortly before serving or stored for weeks in airtight containers, and, if necessary, before they are filled, given a short spell in the oven to regain any lost crispness.

For an 8 inch flan tin allow:

6 *rounded tablespoons self-raising flour*   3 *heaped tablespoons Cake Foundation*

Knead the dough into a ball, and place in the centre of the tin. With floured hands, work this just to cover the flat surface and to fill the surrounding groove.

Bake 25 to 30 minutes in pre-heated oven. (Larger or smaller flans will require longer or shorter times in the oven.)

Cool flan on a wire tray. Fill just before serving. All the fillings given pp. 71–5 are suitable. Fruit Fillings are made in the reverse side of the tin.

Layer Pudding   Oven Setting 375°F, Mark 5

This is made with one of the following fillings, and is good with all of them.

Lemon Fillings, p. 71   *Apple Purée*, p. 132–3
Butterscotch Sauce, p. 80   *Apple Compôte*, p. 134
Butterscotch Crunch, p. 73   *Apple Purée variations*, pp. 72–3
mince meat   *jam or marmalade*

Grease an oven dish or metal pie dish thickly with *butter* and sprinkle with plenty of *sugar*.

Roll a piece of *Cake Foundation Pastry* dough into an oblong (the long side at least twice as long as the short side). Spread liberally with the chosen filling and roll up like a Swiss roll. Place this in the prepared dish, and flatten slightly so that it nearly covers the bottom of the dish. Sprinkle the top with *sugar* and dot with *butter*. Bake 20 to 25 minutes, or till brown, in pre-heated oven. Turn pudding out on to an oven plate or shallow dish and return to the oven for a short while to brown the bottom. Serve hot or cold.

Apple Orange Pudding   Oven Setting 425°F, Mark 7

To serve 5–6 allow:

5 *tablespoons Cake Foundation*   1 *large orange*
10 *tablespoons self-raising flour*   6 *oz sugar, or to taste*
about 1 *lb apples*   ½ *oz butter*

Make a dough with the Foundation and flour. Peel, core and slice the apples. Grate the orange rind and crush it with a little of the sugar. Grease a pie dish with about three quarters of the butter and sprinkle generously with sugar. Line the dish with two thirds of the dough and fill with layers of apple, the rind, and sugar (using most of the remaining sugar). Pour in the orange juice and cover with the remaining dough. Sprinkle on the last of the sugar and dot with the butter.

Bake in pre-heated oven for 30 minutes. Reduce heat to 350°F, Mark 4 and continue to cook until apple is tender and pastry crisp. Turn pudding out on to a large plate and return to the oven for a while to brown the bottom. Serve hot or cold, with *cream* or *custard* (pp. 105, 113).

Note. This pudding is also good made with orthodox short crust pastry.

STEAMED PUDDINGS

When steamed puddings are made with Cake Foundation a delightful light and spongy result is guaranteed.

All the recipes given for baked sponge puddings are equally good when steamed:

Treacle Sponge Pudding (pp. 168–9)   *Jam and Marmalade Sponge Pudding*
Apple Sponge Pudding (p. 169)   (p. 170)
Fruit Sponge Puddings (p. 170)   *Chocolate, Butterscotch,*
     Spice or Lemon Sponge Puddings
     (pp. 170–1)

Turn the batter into a well-greased pudding basin on top of the other given ingredients. Cover with greased paper, aluminium foil or Look and steam for two hours.

Steamed Apple Pudding

For each portion allow:

1 *heaped tablespoon Cake Foundation*	1 *tablespoon shredded,*
1 *rounded tablespoon self-raising flour*	*peeled apple*

Stir the flour and apple into the Cake Foundation. No extra liquid is required. Turn into a well-greased pudding basin, cover with greased paper, aluminium foil or Look and steam for two hours.

Serve with *cream, custard,* a *Hard Sauce* (p. 82) or *a hot Fruit Syrup* (pp. 83–4).

Steamed Pineapple Pudding

For each portion allow:

1 *heaped tablespoon Cake Foundation*	1 *tablespoon finely*
1 *rounded tablespoon self-raising flour*	*chopped tinned pine-*
	apple
	a little pineapple syrup

Mix the Foundation, flour and the pineapple. Add the syrup so that the batter will just drop from the spoon.

Turn into a well-greased basin, cover with greased paper, aluminium foil or Look and steam for two hours.

Steamed Fruit Puddings

To serve 4 allow:

about ½ lb Cake Foundation Pastry	*sugar, honey or*
Dough (pp. 176–7)	*syrup to taste*
1 *lb stewing fruit*	

Cut off one quarter of the dough and set it aside.

Roll the remainder to a thickness of about ¼ inch. With this, line a well-greased pudding basin. Pack firmly with the fruit, adding sweetening between the layers.

For the cover, roll out the dough which has been set aside. Lay this on the fruit, press it down and pinch the edges together. Cover with greased paper, aluminium foil or Look and steam for two hours.

EVAPORATED MILK

INEXPENSIVE and delicious Mousses (savoury and sweet), Ice Creams and other Cold Sweets can be made with tins of evaporated milk, which have been boiled and then chilled for at least 12 hours. This milk will whip up to more than twice its original quantity, and at the same time the strong flavour to which many people object is reduced. Thus, when other flavours are added, any remaining tang is disguised.

It is true that evaporated milk which has been chilled without previous boiling will also whip up, but not to the same extent, nor as thickly.

Place the tins, unpierced, in a pan of water and boil for 15 minutes. Do not leave the kitchen during this process, unless you have an infallible memory or a timer; should the boiling time be forgotten and the pan boil dry, there would be a most unpleasant explosion. Cool the boiled tins and store them in a refrigerator, where they can remain indefinitely.

Most of the following recipes are for boiled and chilled small tins of evaporated milk, but all these can be adapted for a large tin, which holds as much milk as 2⅓ small tins. *Thus to increase the given recipe, use a large tin and just over double all the other ingredients.*

COLD SAVOURIES, SWEETS *and* ICE CREAMS

Savoury Mousses

Salmon Mousse

To serve 4–6 allow:

7–8 *oz tin red salmon*	1 *dessertspoon gelatine* soaked in
2 *tablespoons Mayonnaise*	1 *tablespoon cold water*
(p. 98)	2 *tablespoons boiling water*
1 *teaspoon lemon juice*	*small tin evaporated milk*
a little freshly milled pepper	(boiled and chilled)

Place salmon in a basin with the Mayonnaise, lemon juice and pepper. Mash well with a fork.

Dissolve the soaked gelatine with the boiling water and stir into the salmon.

Whip the milk until thick. As the salmon begins to set, fold into the whipped milk.

Transfer to serving bowl. Chill well. Serve with *lettuce and sliced cucumber.*

Tuna Fish Mousse

To serve 6 allow:

two 6 *oz tins of tuna fish*
1 *dessertspoon finely chopped onion*
½ *clove garlic* (crushed)
juice of ½ a lemon
1 *dessertspoon brandy or*
  sherry (optional)

2 *tablespoons olive oil*
salt and pepper to taste
1 *dessertspoon powdered gelatine*
  soaked in
1 *tablespoon cold water*
2 *tablespoons boiling water*
small tin evaporated milk
  (boiled and chilled)

Place all the ingredients other than the milk, gelatine and water in a bowl and mash with a fork. Make this mixture into a purée, either in a liquidizer or in a Moulin-Legumes (using the finest disc).

Dissolve the soaked gelatine in the boiling water. Whip the milk until thick, then fold in the fish purée and dissolved gelatine.

Pour into 1 large dish or 6 individual bowls for serving. Chill.

Kipper Mousse

To serve 4–5 allow:

a 7 *oz tin kipper fillets or*
4 *cooked kipper fillets*
juice of ½ lemon
1 *dessertspoon gelatine* soaked in
1 *tablespoon cold water*

2 *tablespoons boiling water*
small tin evaporated milk
  (boiled and chilled)
freshly milled pepper
sliced lemon

Purée the kipper fillets either in an electric blender or by passing them through a Moulinette or a fine sieve. Add the lemon juice.

Dissolve the soaked gelatine with the boiling water.

Whip the milk until thick. Fold in the kipper purée and dissolved gelatine and season with pepper.

Pour into serving bowl or individual dishes. Chill.

Before serving, decorate with *sliced lemon.*

Ham or Tongue Mousse

To serve 4 allow:

6 *oz minced ham or tongue*   1 *dessertspoon gelatine* soaked in
1 *teaspoon French or English*   1 *tablespoon cold stock*
   mustard   3 *tablespoons boiling stock*
a pinch garlic powder (optional)   *small tin evaporated milk*
          (boiled and chilled)

Place the minced ham or tongue in a basin with the mustard and garlic powder.

Dissolve the soaked gelatine with the boiling stock and stir into the meat.

Whip the milk until thick. As the meat begins to set, fold in the whipped milk.

Transfer to a serving bowl. Chill well before serving.

Paté de Foie Mousse

To serve 6 allow:

two 4 *oz tins Paté de Foie*   2 *tablespoons boiling water*
1 *tablespoon sherry*   *small tin evaporated milk*
1 *tablespoon brandy*   (boiled and chilled)
½ *teaspoon lemon juice*   *salt and freshly milled pepper*
1 *dessertspoon gelatine* soaked in
1 *tablespoon cold water*

Place the paté in a basin. Stir in the sherry, brandy and lemon juice.

Dissolve the soaked gelatine with the boiling water and stir into the paté.

Whip the milk until thick. As the paté begins to set, fold it into the whipped milk. Season to taste.

Chill well.

Place on lettuce leaves, and serve with *thin slices of brown bread and butter.*

Cottage Cheese and Pepper Mousse

To serve 6 allow:

8 *oz carton cottage cheese*   2 *tablespoons boiling water*
1 *green pepper*   *small tin evaporated milk*
1 *dessertspoon gelatine* soaked in   (boiled and chilled)
1 *tablespoon cold water*   1 *teaspoon lemon juice*
          salt and freshly milled pepper
             to taste

Place the cottage cheese in a basin.

Wash the pepper, cut in half, remove the seeds, slice finely and add to the cottage cheese.

Dissolve the soaked gelatine with the boiling water and stir into the cheese.

Whip the milk until thick. As the cottage cheese mixture begins to set, fold into the whipped milk. Stir in the lemon juice and seasoning. Transfer to serving bowl.

Chill well before serving.

Egg Mousse 2 (Egg Mousse 1, p. 106)

To serve 6 allow:

6 *hard boiled eggs*, sliced	*small tin evaporated milk*
10 *oz tin consommé soup*	(boiled and chilled)
	salt and pepper to taste

Blend the sliced eggs with the consommé soup, either in an electric blender, or through a fine sieve.

Whip the evaporated milk until very thick. Fold in the egg mixture and season.

Transfer to serving bowl and chill well in the refrigerator. Before serving decorate with *slices of tomato and cucumber*.

Sweet Mousses

Apricot Mousse

To serve 4–5 allow:

a 15–16 *oz tin apricots* (strained)	4 *tablespoons boiling syrup*
1 *dessertspoon gelatine* soaked in	1 *small tin evaporated milk*
1 *tablespoon cold apricot syrup*	(boiled and chilled)
	1 *tablespoon caster sugar*

Dissolve the soaked gelatine in the boiling apricot syrup.

Chop or liquidize most of the fruit, leaving enough for decoration.

Whip the milk until thick. Fold in the fruit, sugar and dissolved gelatine.

Pour into serving bowl. Chill.

Before serving, decorate with *whipped cream* (p. 105) and slices of apricot.

Banana Mousse

To serve 4–5 allow:

4 *or* 5 *bananas*	1 *dessertspoon powdered gelatine*
juice of 1 *lemon*	soaked in
3 *oz caster sugar*	1 *tablespoon cold water*
1 *small tin evaporated milk*	2 *tablespoons boiling water*
(boiled and chilled)	

Mash the bananas until smooth with the lemon juice and sugar, either by hand or in a liquidizer.

Whip the evaporated milk until thick.

Dissolve the soaked gelatine with the boiling water and stir into the milk.

Lastly fold in the banana mixture.

Pour into a serving bowl and leave until set.

Decorate with *whipped cream* (p. 105).

Lemon Mousse

To serve 4–5 allow:

1 *dessertspoon gelatine* soaked in	*small tin evaporated milk*
1 *tablespoon lemon juice*	(boiled and chilled)
grated rind of 1 *lemon*	3 *tablespoons caster sugar*
	2 *fluid oz boiling lemon juice*

Whip the milk together with the lemon rind and sugar.

Dissolve the soaked gelatine with the boiling lemon juice and stir it gradually into the whipped milk.

Turn quickly into serving dish or sundae glasses.

Decorate with *whipped cream* (p. 105) and *grated chocolate* or *glacé cherries* before serving.

Pineapple Mousse

To serve 4–5 allow:

a 13–15 *oz tin crushed pineapple*	*small tin evaporated milk*
(strained)	(boiled and chilled)
1 *dessertspoon gelatine* soaked in	1 *tablespoon caster sugar*
1 *tablespoon cold pineapple syrup*	1 *teaspoon lemon juice*
3 *tablespoons boiling syrup*	

Dissolve the soaked gelatine with the boiling pineapple syrup.

Whip the milk until thick. Fold in the dissolved gelatine, crushed pineapple, caster sugar and lemon juice.

Pour into serving bowl and chill.

Decorate with *whipped cream* (p. 105).

Raspberry Mousse (*made from tinned raspberries*)

To serve 4–5 allow:

a 15 *oz tin raspberries* (strained)	4 *tablespoons boiling syrup*
1 *dessertspoon gelatine* soaked in	*small tin evaporated milk*
1 *tablespoon cold raspberry syrup*	(boiled and chilled)
	1 *tablespoon caster sugar*

Add the boiling raspberry syrup to the soaked gelatine, and stir until dissolved.

Mash the fruit and remaining syrup.

Whip the milk until thick. Fold in sugar, fruit and dissolved gelatine.

Pour into serving bowl. Chill.

Serve decorated with *whipped cream* (p. 105).

Fresh Fruit Mousse (made with an electric liquidizer)

To serve 6 allow:

1 *lb fresh soft fruit*	2 *tablespoons boiling water*
12 *tablespoons caster sugar*	1 *small tin evaporated milk*
1 *dessertspoon gelatine* soaked in	(boiled and chilled)
1 *tablespoon cold water*	

Liquidize the fruit with the sugar and pour into large mixing bowl.

Dissolve the soaked gelatine with the boiling water and stir into the fruit purée.

Whip the evaporated milk until very thick, then fold it into the fruit.

Pour into serving bowl or sundae glasses.

Chill before serving.

Top with a little *whipped cream* (p. 105).

Coffee Mousse

To serve 4–5 allow:

1 *dessertspoon gelatine* soaked in	2 *tablespoons caster sugar*
1 *tablespoon cold coffee*	1½ *fluid oz boiling coffee*
small tin evaporated milk	
(boiled and chilled)	

C.A.—G

Whip the evaporated milk and sugar until thick.

Dissolve the soaked gelatine with the boiling coffee, then stir it into the milk.

Turn quickly into the dish or glasses in which the mousse is to be served.

Immediately before serving decorate with *whipped cream* (p. 105) and *nuts.*

Coffee Chocolate Mousse

As for *Coffee Mousse*, with the addition of 2 *tablespoons cocoa*, to be added to the milk with the sugar.

Caramel Mousse

To serve 4–5 allow:

1 *dessertspoon gelatine* soaked in	*small tin evaporated milk*
1 *tablespoon cold water*	(boiled and chilled)
1 *tablespoon boiling Caramel*	3 *tablespoons Caramel Syrup*
Syrup (p. 79)	

Pour boiling Caramel Syrup over the soaked gelatine and stir until the gelatine is dissolved.

Whip the milk until thick. Fold in the gelatine and cold caramel syrup.

Pour into serving bowl. Chill.

Ginger Mousse

To serve 4–5 allow:

½ *teaspoon ground ginger* and	*small tin evaporated milk*
1 *dessertspoon gelatine* soaked in	(boiled and chilled)
1 *tablespoon cold water*	2 *tablespoons caster sugar*
1½ *fluid oz boiling water*	4 *oz chopped preserved or*
	crystallized ginger

Dissolve the soaked ginger and gelatine with the boiling water.

Whip the milk and sugar until thick. Fold in the dissolved ginger and gelatine and most of the chopped preserved ginger.

Pour into serving bowl. Chill.

Before serving, top with *whipped cream* (p. 105) and decorate with the remaining preserved ginger.

Russes and Creams

Sherry Charlotte Russe

To serve 6 allow:

8 *sponge cakes*	*a small tin evaporated milk*
9 *tablespoons sherry*	(boiled and chilled)
1½ *teaspoons gelatine* soaked in	1 *tablespoon caster sugar*
1 *dessertspoon sherry*	*whipped cream* (p. 105)
2 *tablespoons boiling water*	*glacé cherries*
	blanched almonds

Halve sponge cakes horizontally. Line a soufflé dish or cake tin 7 inches in diameter with the crisper halves. Sprinkle with 4 tablespoons of sherry.

Crumble the balance of the sponge cake into a basin and pour over it the remaining 5 tablespoons of sherry.

Add the boiling water to the soaked gelatine and stir until the gelatine is dissolved.

Whip milk until very thick. Fold it slowly into the gelatine, soaked crumbs and sugar.

Pour the mixture into the cake-lined mould. If necessary trim the cake to match the centre. Chill.

Before serving, unmould the russe and decorate with whipped cream, glacé cherries and blanched almonds.

Peach and Sherry Russe

To serve 6 allow:

8 *sponge cakes*	1 *dessertspoon gelatine* soaked in
1 *large tin sliced peaches*	2 *tablespoons cold syrup*
3 *tablespoons sherry*	*small tin evaporated milk*
	(boiled and chilled)

Cut sponge cakes in half horizontally. Line a soufflé dish or a cake tin 7 inches in diameter with the crisper halves.

Strain the peaches over a basin. Stir the sherry into the syrup, and sprinkle about 5 tablespoons over the sponge-lined mould.

Dissolve the soaked gelatine in *about 4 tablespoons boiling syrup.*

Crumble the remaining sponge cakes into a basin and pour over the rest of the syrup.

Cut up most of the peaches (leaving a few for decoration) and stir into the soaked sponge.

Whip milk until thick. Fold it slowly into the gelatine, sponge and peach mixture.

Pour mixture into cake-lined mould. Chill.

Before serving, unmould, and decorate with *whipped cream* (p. 105) and sliced peaches.

Orange Cointreau Russe

To serve 6 allow:

8 *sponge cakes*	1½ *teaspoons gelatine* soaked in
juice of 2 *oranges*	1 *dessertspoon orange squash*
4 *liqueur glasses Cointreau*	2 *tablespoons boiling orange squash*
grated rind of 1 *orange*	*small tin evaporated milk*
	(boiled and chilled)

Halve the sponge cakes horizontally. Line a soufflé dish or cake tin 7 inches in diameter with the crisper halves.

Mix the orange juice with the Cointreau.

Crumble the balance of the sponge cakes into a basin and pour over it half the Cointreau mixture. Add the grated orange rind.

Sprinkle the remaining Cointreau over the sponge-lined mould.

Add the boiling squash to the soaked gelatine and stir until dissolved.

Whip the milk until very thick. Fold it slowly into the gelatine and soaked crumbs.

Pour the mixture into the cake-lined mould. If necessary, trim the cake to match the centre. Chill.

Before serving, unmould the russe and decorate with *whipped cream* (p. 105).

Chocolate Sherry Cream

To serve 6–8 allow:

4 *sponge cakes*	8 *fluid oz boiling water*
4 *tablespoons sherry*	¼ *lb plain chocolate*
1 *tablespoon instant coffee*	2 *tablespoons milk*
1 *tablespoon gelatine*	*small tin evaporated milk*
2 *tablespoons cold water*	(boiled and chilled)
	2 *egg whites*

Roughly crumble the sponge cakes into a large bowl. Pour over the sherry.

Put the coffee, gelatine and cold water in a basin and leave to soak

for a few minutes. Dissolve this with the boiling water before pouring
it over the sponge cakes.

Break chocolate into a small pan. Add the milk and melt slowly
without boiling. Stir into the sponge cake mixture.

Leave in a cool place for about 15 minutes or until it is beginning to
set.

Whip up the evaporated milk until thick and fold into the setting
chocolate coffee sponge.

Lastly fold in the stiffly beaten egg whites.

Chill well.

Decorate with *whipped cream* (p. 105) *and walnuts.*

Orange Rum Cream

To serve 6 allow:

5 *oranges*	1 *tablespoon gelatine* soaked in
2 *tablespoons sugar*	2 *tablespoons cold water*
4 *sponge cakes*	5 *tablespoons boiling water*
3 *fluid oz rum*	*small tin evaporated milk*
	(boiled and chilled)

Before peeling and removing all the pith from four of the oranges,
grate the rind off two of them on to a plate. Squeeze the juice out of the
fifth orange. Measure the sugar on to the plate, and crush it into the rind
with a wooden spoon. Tip this orange sugar mixture into a small
saucepan.

Crumble the sponge cakes into a basin, and pour on to them the rum
and orange juice. Toss the crumbs lightly with a fork, so that they
become impregnated without getting too mushy.

Add the boiling water to the peel and sugar in the pan, bring to the
boil again, and mix it with the soaked gelatine. Mix well.

Cut the peeled oranges, on a plate, into thin horizontal slices. Save
the juice but discard the pips. Transfer fruit and juice to the basin with
the gelatine mixture. Rotate slices so that they are well coated. Leave for
10 minutes. Then with a fork, take out the slices, one by one, and
arrange them on the bottom and against the sides of a round or square
bowl.

Whip up the milk. Then gradually fold in, first the orange jelly, then
the sponge cake mixture, and pour into the bowl on top of the orange
slices.

Chill. Before serving, unmould on to a dish and decorate with *whipped
cream* (p. 105).

Ice Creams

This home-made ice cream may not be quite as creamy as that produced by Messrs Walls and Lyons; yet it certainly is good, versatile, quick and easy to prepare and useful to have 'on tap'.

The ice cream can either be stored in the refrigerator trays or dishes in which it was made, or, when beginning to freeze, whisked again and transferred to containers, large, or small individual ones, to be stored in a deep freeze.

As ice cream keeps for weeks, just in a refrigerator, it is more practical to make the larger quantity, provided the freezing compartment is adequate. The following recipes are therefore given for the large tins of evaporated milk.

When only a little ice cream is wanted, adapt these recipes by using a small tin and just under half all the other given ingredients.

Vanilla Ice Cream

1¼ teaspoons powdered gelatine soaked in
1 tablespoon cold water
3 tablespoons boiling water

a large tin evaporated milk (boiled and chilled)
3 tablespoons caster sugar
1½ teaspoons vanilla

Dissolve the soaked gelatine with the boiling water.

Whip the evaporated milk together with the sugar until light and thick. Towards the end of the whipping, gradually add the dissolved gelatine and finally the vanilla.

Pour into refrigerator trays or dishes and place in the freezing compartment.

Vanilla Ice Cream is used in:

Coffee Ice Cream 2 (p. 191)
Chocolate Ice Cream (p. 191)
Caramel Ice Cream (p. 191)
Nut-brittle Ice Cream (pp. 192–3)
Sundaes (pp. 193–5)
Banana Splits (p. 195)
Pastry Slices and Horns (pp. 60, 42)
Orange and Raspberry Delights (pp. 171–2)

Coffee Ice Cream 1

1¼ *teaspoons gelatine* soaked in
1 *tablespoon cold coffee or water*
3 *tablespoons boiling coffee*

1 *large tin evaporated milk*
(boiled and chilled)
2½ *tablespoons caster sugar*
Camp Coffee to taste

Dissolve the soaked gelatine in the boiling coffee.

Whip the milk together with the sugar until light and thick, adding the coffee and gelatine towards the end of the whipping. Stir in the Camp Coffee.

Pour into refrigerator trays or other dishes and place in the freezing compartment.

Coffee Ice Cream 2

Vanilla Ice Cream (p. 190)   *Camp Coffee*

This is made by adding the coffee to the Ice Cream just as it is beginning to freeze and whipping it in with a whisk or a fork and returning it to the freezing compartment.

The advantage of this method is that as much or as little as is wanted of the Vanilla Ice Cream can be transformed into Coffee Ice Cream.

Coffee Ice Cream is used in:

Coffee Sundaes (p, 194) and **Coffee Nut Brittle** (pp. 192–3)

Chocolate Ice Cream

Vanilla Ice Cream (p. 190)
1 *oz butter or margarine*
2 *level tablespoons cocoa*

2 *tablespoons milk*
1½–2 *tablespoons caster sugar*

When the Ice Cream is beginning to freeze, put all the other ingredients in a small saucepan over very gentle heat. Stir until well blended, but do not allow to boil.

Add sauce to Ice Cream and whip it in with a fork or whisk.

Return to freezing compartment.

Chocolate Ice Cream is used in:

Chocolate Sundaes (p. 194) and **Chocolate Nut Brittle** (p. 192)

Caramel Ice Cream

Vanilla Ice Cream (p. 194)   8 *tablespoons Caramel Syrup* (p. 192)

Just before freezing, fold in the caramel syrup.

Caramel Sundaes, p. 194

Strawberry or Raspberry Ice Cream 1

1¾ *teaspoons gelatine* soaked in
1 *tablespoon cold water*
14 *oz fruit*
8–10 *tablespoons caster sugar*

2 *tablespoons hot water*
a large tin evaporated milk
(boiled and chilled)

Crush the fruit and sugar with the hot water and tip it into a sieve, placed over a saucepan, to drain. Boil the resulting liquid and pour it over the soaked gelatine. Stir until dissolved.

Transfer the fruit from the sieve to the pan and just bring to the boil, before returning it to the sieve, and working it through until only the pips remain.

Add gelatine and juice to the fruit.

Whip the milk until thick and gradually fold it into the fruit mixture.

Pour into refrigerator trays or dishes and place in the freezing compartment.

Strawberry or Raspberry Ice Cream 2 (made in an electric liquidizer)

1¾ *teaspoons gelatine* soaked in
1 *tablespoon cold water*
2¼ *tablespoons boiling water*
14 *oz fruit*

8–10 *tablespoons sugar*
a large tin evaporated milk
(boiled and chilled)

Dissolve the soaked gelatine in the boiling water.

Put the fruit, sugar and gelatine in a liquidizer and liquidize at high speed for half a minute.

Whip up milk until light and thick. Gradually fold this into the fruit mixture.

Pour into refrigerator trays or dishes and place in the freezing compartment.

Nut-brittle Ice Cream

Vanilla, Coffee or Chocolate
Ice Cream (pp. 190–1)

½ *lb nut-brittle, broken*
into small pieces

All three of these Ice Creams make a delicious Nut-brittle Ice, though possibly Coffee Nut-brittle Ice Cream is the general favourite.

When the Ice Cream is just beginning to freeze, add the brittle and whip it in with a fork before returning it to the freezing compartment.

Of course not all the original Ice Cream need be transformed, in which case reduce the nut-brittle proportionately.

Nut-brittle Sundaes, p. 195

Chocolate Peppermint Ice Cream

1½ teaspoons gelatine soaked in
1 tablespoon cold water
3 tablespoons boiling water
a large tin evaporated milk
   (boiled and chilled)

3 tablespoons caster sugar
a few drops peppermint essence
a few drops green colouring
   (optional)

Prepare as given for *Vanilla Ice Cream* (p. 190), substituting the peppermint for the vanilla, and when this is beginning to freeze, add:

½ lb Elizabeth Shaw's Chocolate Peppermint Crisps, broken into small pieces

Whip with a fork and return the ice cream to the freezing compartment.

Chocolate Peppermint Sundae, p. 195

Ice Cream Sundaes

These are sweets made with Ice Cream (main ingredient), a sauce, whipped cream (p. 105) and harmonizing additions.

Vanilla Sundaes

Use: *Vanilla Ice Cream*, p. 190

Sauces:

Butterscotch, p. 80
Chocolate 1 and 2, pp. 79, 80
Coffee, p. 81
Caramel Syrup, p. 79

Spice, p. 81
Orange, p. 88
Fruit Syrups, p. 83

Additions:

chopped nuts
   with *Butterscotch* or *Chocolate Sauces* or *Caramel Syrup.*

fresh fruit
>*Fruit Syrup* and *Orange Sauce* blend well with fresh fruits, but when the fruit is soaked in sugar to which a little alcohol can be added, no other sauce is necessary.

tinned fruit
>use the syrup from the tin, to which can be added one of the *Fruit Syrups* or a little alcohol.

ginger, preserved or crystallized
>use the syrup from preserved ginger and *Spice Sauce* with crystallized ginger.

Coffee Sundaes

Use: *Coffee Ice Cream* 1 *or* 2, p. 191

>Sauces:
>
>| | |
>|---|---|
>| *Coffee*, p. 81 | *Caramel*, p. 79 |
>| *Chocolate* 1 *or* 2, pp. 79, 80 | |
>
>Additions:
>
>| | | |
>|---|---|---|
>| *chopped nuts* | *glacé cherries* | *grated chocolate* |

Chocolate Sundaes

Use: *Chocolate Ice Cream*, p. 191

>Sauces:
>
>| | |
>|---|---|
>| *Chocolate* 1 *or* 2, p. 79, 80 | *Orange Syrup*, p. 83 |
>| *Orange Brandy*, p. 81 | |
>
>Additions:
>
>| | |
>|---|---|
>| *chopped nuts* | *candied peel* |
>| *glacé cherries* | *crystallized fruit* |

Caramel Sundaes

Use: *Caramel Ice Cream*, p. 191

>Sauce:
>
>>*Caramel Syrup* p. 79
>
>Addition:
>
>>*chopped nuts*

Strawberry or Raspberry Sundaes

Use: *Strawberry or Raspberry Ice Cream*, p. 192.

Make the sauce by cutting up some *strawberries or raspberries* and soaking them for a while with *caster or icing sugar*. Then add *a little sherry, kirsch, white wine or water* and either sieve or liquidize the mixture.

Place a few of the best berries on top of the *whipped cream.*

Nut-brittle Sundaes

Use: *Nut-brittle Ice Cream,* pp. 192–3, either Vanilla, Coffee or Chocolate.

Sauces:

Butterscotch, p. 80	*Coffee,* p. 81
Chocolate 1 *or* 2, pp. 79, 80	*Caramel Syrup* p. 79

Additions:

chopped nuts

Chocolate Peppermint Sundae

Use: *Chocolate Peppermint Ice Cream,* p. 193

Sauce:

Chocolate 1 *or* 2, pp. 79, 80

Addition:

grated plain chocolate

Banana Splits

Bananas	*raspberry jam*
Vanilla Ice Cream, p. 190	*whipped cream,* p. 105

Slice the bananas in half lengthwise. Spread with jam and sandwich together with Ice Cream. Top with cream.

Ginger Delights

These excellent sweets are quickly assembled, immediately before serving, in individual fruit bowls.

For each Delight allow:

2 *Gingersnaps,* p. 161.	*whipped cream,* p. 105
a slice of Vanilla Ice Cream	*a few pieces chopped*
p. 190	*preserved ginger*
about 2 tablespoons Spice	
Sauce or Syrup, p. 81	

Place the ice cream between the gingersnaps. Pour over the sauce, or preserved ginger syrup, and top with cream and ginger.

WHOLEWHEAT BREAD, ROLLS
AND BUN LOAVES

SOME home-made bread, rolls and bun loaves are likely to be welcomed by the many who consider bought bread is not nearly as good as it used to be, yet cannot spare the time to by-pass the baker altogether.

Wholewheat Meal Bread   Oven setting – lowest possible

Nothing could be simpler to make than this excellent loaf. It has a lovely nutty flavour, keeps fresh for days and then makes delicious toast. The original recipe stipulated 'stone ground' flour; Allinson makes this, but some may prefer an equally good and somewhat lighter loaf made with Rank's wholewheat meal.

To make a good 2 lb loaf allow:

$1\frac{1}{2}$ *lbs wholewheat meal*	17 *fluid oz tepid water*
$\frac{1}{2}$ *oz salt*	*a good $\frac{1}{2}$ oz baker's yeast*
$\frac{1}{2}$ *oz soft brown sugar*	*or a good $\frac{1}{4}$ oz dried yeast*
	($1\frac{1}{4}$–$1\frac{1}{2}$ *teaspoons*)

Place the meal and salt in a large mixing bowl.

Put the sugar in a small basin, pour over it about 4 fluid oz of the measured water and add the yeast. Work the baker's yeast into the sugar with a wooden spoon, or sprinkle in the dried yeast.

Grease a 2 lb loaf tin.

Put in the ultra-cool oven: the mixing bowl, the small basin, covered with a cloth, the loaf tin and the rest of the water, and leave 10 to 15 minutes, until the sugar, water and yeast are completely blended. Remove all but the tin.

Make a well in the meal and pour into it the yeast mixture.

Gradually add the water, working it in with a palette or pliable knife. When all the meal is moistened, knead the dough until it does not stick to the hands or the mixing bowl – if necessary add a little extra meal.

Turn the dough into the warm tin and bake for 45 minutes.

Without opening the oven door, increase heat to 400°F, Mark 6, and bake for a further 45 minutes.

Rolls

These will be appreciated by all who enjoy hot rolls for breakfast. Stored in a Tupperware container or in a polythene bag which is kept in the refrigerator, the rolls will keep for a week, and of course for many weeks in a deep freeze.

To reheat and restore freshness, place rolls in a paper bag and leave in a hot oven for 10 to 15 minutes.

To make 12 rolls allow:

1 *lb plain flour*	½ *oz baker's yeast or* ¼ *oz dried yeast*
¼ *teaspoon salt*	(1¼ *teaspoons*)
½ *oz caster sugar*	½ *pint tepid milk*
	1 *oz melted butter*

Sieve the flour and salt into a mixing bowl, and place the sugar in a small basin.

When using baker's yeast, cream this into the sugar until liquid, then add about 4 fluid oz of the lukewarm milk. Cover basin with a cloth.

When using dried yeast, pour about 4 fluid oz of the warm milk over the sugar and sprinkle in the yeast. Cover basin with a cloth.

Add the melted butter to the remaining milk and put it, the yeast mixture and the flour in a warm place – a plate oven or a heated airing cupboard – for 10 to 15 minutes.

Now make a well in the flour and pour in the yeast mixture.

Gradually add the milk and butter, working it in with a palette or pliable knife and then kneading it. Continue to knead until the dough is very smooth and pliable and no longer sticks to the hands or the mixing bowl. During this process, a little extra flour may be sifted over the dough and the hands.

Cover the bowl with a cloth and return the dough to the warm place for 45 minutes or until it has risen to quite double its original size.

Knead the dough again for a few minutes, then cut it into 12 equal portions. Knead each of these before shaping into balls and placing them, about 3 inches apart, on warm floured baking sheets.

Turn on the oven, 400°F, Mark 6, and return the rolls to the warm place for 15 minutes to prove.

Bake 15 to 20 minutes.

Hot Cross Buns

To make 12 buns allow:

1 *lb plain flour*	4 *oz currants*
¼ *teaspoon each salt, ginger,*	½ *oz baker's yeast or* ¼ *oz dried*
nutmeg, cinnamon	*yeast* (1¼ *teaspoons*)
a pinch powdered cloves	½ *pint tepid milk*
2½ *oz caster sugar*	1½ *oz melted butter*

Sieve the flour, salt, spices and 2 oz sugar into a mixing bowl. Add the currants.

Place the remaining sugar in a small basin.

Continue as given for *Rolls* except, before baking, dissolve

1 *tablespoon sugar* in 1 *tablespoon water*

Brush the buns with this before marking with a cross, using the back of a knife.

Croissants

To make 8–10 croissants allow:

8 *oz plain flour*	¼ *pint tepid milk*
pinch of salt	4 *oz butter*
1 *teaspoon sugar*	*a little extra milk or*
½ *oz baker's yeast or*	*beaten egg*
¼ *oz dried yeast* (1¼ *teaspoons*)	

Sieve flour and salt into a mixing bowl, and place the sugar in a small basin.

When using baker's yeast, cream this into the sugar, add the tepid milk and cover with a cloth.

When using dried yeast, pour the tepid milk over the sugar, sprinkle in the yeast and cover with a cloth.

Leave the flour and the yeast mixture in a warm place – a plate oven or a heated airing cupboard – for 10 to 15 minutes.

Pour the yeast mixture into the flour and mix well.

Cover bowl with a cloth and return to the warm place for about an hour, when the dough should be approximately double its original size.

Turn on to a floured board and knead lightly, then roll into an oblong shape. Place one third of the butter, cut into small pieces, on to the dough. Fold as for flaky pastry, turn and roll out again. Repeat twice, using the rest of the butter.

Roll out thinly, cut in half lengthwise, then cut each strip into 4 or 5 large triangles. Starting at the base, roll up each triangle and form into a crescent. Place these on ungreased baking sheets and return to the warm place for about 20 minutes to prove.

Turn on oven, 425°F, Mark 7.

Brush croissants with milk or beaten egg before putting them in the hot oven. Bake about 15 minutes.

Bun Loaf   Oven Setting 350°F, Mark 4

2 cups (16 *fluid oz*) *self-raising flour*   1 *pinch salt*
1 *tablespoon sugar*   3–4 *tablespoons dried fruit*
1 *tablespoon golden syrup*   1 *egg*

Mix the ingredients together in a large bowl. Add enough milk to make a dough the consistency of a cake batter.

Turn into a greased 2 lb loaf tin.

Bake for ¾ hour in pre-heated oven.

Serve in slices spread with butter.

Bun loaf is rarely allowed to get stale. If it does, it is delicious toasted and eaten hot with lashings of butter.

Bran Loaf   Oven Setting 350°F, Mark 4

In this recipe quantities are given in cups, so that the size of cup used can regulate the size of the loaf. This may prove useful.

1 *cup All Bran*   1 *cup milk*
1 *cup sugar*   1 *egg* (small or large according to size of cup)
1 *cup dried fruit*   1 *cup self-raising flour*

Mix together in a bowl the All Bran, sugar, dried fruit and milk. Leave all night to soak.

Next day add the egg and flour. Stir well.

Turn into a greased loaf tin.

Bake for 45 minutes.

When cold, slice and butter.

Brack Bun Loaf   Oven Setting 300°F, Mark 2

1 *lb mixed dried fruit*   16 *fluid oz self-raising flour*
8 *fluid oz soft dark brown sugar*   *pinch of each of mixed spice and*
8 *fluid oz strong tea*   *nutmeg*
   (without milk or sugar)   1 *egg, well beaten*

Place the fruit in a bowl and cover with the sugar and tea. Leave overnight.

The following morning, add the flour, spices and egg.

Mix well and turn into a well greased 2 lb loaf tin.

Bake in coolest oven position for about 2 hours.

When quite cold, wrap in grease-proof paper and leave until the next day. This loaf keeps fresh for days, and in fact improves with keeping.

Serve in slices spread with butter.

Malt Loaf   Oven Setting 400°F, Mark 6

16 *fluid oz self-raising flour*
5 *tablespoons sugar*
1 *tablespoon golden syrup*
5 *tablespoons raisins*

1½ *tablespoons Ovaltine*
about 4 *fluid oz boiling water*
¼ *pint milk*
1 *teaspoon bicarbonate soda*

Grease a 2 lb loaf tin.

Put the flour, sugar, syrup and fruit in a mixing bowl and the Ovaltine in a measure. Pour boiling water over the Ovaltine up to the 4 fluid oz mark, blend well, and add the milk.

Gradually stir the liquid into the other ingredients, leaving about 1 fluid oz in the measure. Mix well.

Lastly, dissolve the bicarbonate in the remaining liquid and stir it into the mixture.

Pour the batter into the loaf tin and bake in pre-heated oven for an hour.

Serve in slices spread with butter.

Malt Loaf keeps fresh for some while, but is also good toasted.

Browned Breadcrumbs

Stale bread, crusts, spurned toast, all make excellent browned bread-crumbs and should never be wasted, but saved and baked whenever there is room for them in a cool oven.

Once baked, they need not be turned into crumbs immediately, but can be stored again – paper bags will do – until the next time a grater, shredder or mincer is in action. Then grate, shred or mince them as finely as possible, and store in an airtight tin.

Both browned and fresh breadcrumbs are useful for quickly thicken-ing sauces and soups and need no extra cooking.

In an emergency, they can also be added to dishes that are too fatty. They will absorb the fat and make little difference to the flavour.

Fresh Breadcrumbs

Fresh white breadcrumbs are quickly made from stale bread, in a liquidizer, on a good grater or through the fine disc of a Mouli Shredder. These will be found better for egg and crumbing than the browned crumbs; the result is crisper and the colour more attractive.

Sweet Fried Crumbs

A supply of these crumbs in your store cupboard is always an asset. They are not only an essential ingredient of the delicious *Danish Apple Cake*, but are also good when sprinkled over fruit and cold sweets.

> 15 *fluid oz Browned Breadcrumbs*   6 *oz caster sugar*
> 3 *oz butter or margarine*   1–2 *teaspoons cinnamon* (optional)

Put all the ingredients into a warmed, large, heavy frying pan and place over very gentle heat. Stir constantly, and often scrape the crumbs from the bottom of the pan to prevent burning.

After about 10 to 15 minutes, the crumbs should have absorbed the fat and be brown and crisp.

Cover a wire tray with absorbent paper and tip the crumbs on to it.

When cold, store in a screw top jar or any other airtight container: the crumbs will keep for months.

INDEX